The Port Hudson Campaign

The Port Hudson Campaign

1862-1863

BY EDWARD CUNNINGHAM

Louisiana State University Press
Baton Rouge and London

Foreword

SOMETIMES an event or an episode in history gets "lost." It is remembered as a name and is mentioned in the books as something that happened. But its reality and significance disappear, and only the name survives. Usually this slide into oblivion occurs when one episode is a part of a larger one and is overshadowed by the more spectacular action. It happens most frequently in military history, which deals in campaigns of related battles, with the result that an engagement of real importance may be completely overlooked because the "lookers," the historians and writers, are obsessed with something else that seems more important.

Oblivion has been the undeserved fate of one of the most interesting operations of our Civil War, an operation that took place in Louisiana—the siege of Port Hudson in 1863. Port Hudson had the bad historical luck to be caught up in the great Vicksburg campaign, and the battles around the Mississippi fortress have almost completely eclipsed the actions at the Louisiana stronghold. All accounts of the war stress, as they should, the Vicksburg story. Almost as a footnote, they add that after Vicksburg fell Port Hudson surrendered. The impression given is that Port Hudson was a mere side show, that nothing that happened there could conceivably have influenced the outcome of the struggle for the Mississippi River. But a minute's cogitation will convince anyone that the common opinion is wrong. The two river towns were parts of a related defense system, and their fortunes were inextricably connected. It is true that after Vicksburg yielded, Port Hudson had to yield. But what if Port Hudson had fallen first? Then the Federal army there could have been free to join the Federals farther up the river, and Vicksburg would have fallen sooner than it did. What the results of such a contingency would have been we cannot with certainty say. We can surmise, however, that the course of the war would have been altered. The Confederates at Port Hudson, by their dogged resistance, stalled the Union victory schedule and thereby prolonged the conflict.

An additional reason for the obscurity of the Port Hudson campaign is that hitherto not very much has been known about it. It has never been the subject of a systematic and scholarly study. Now it receives that kind of treatment in Edward Cunningham's monograph. Mr. Cunningham is a young scholar, presently a graduate student at Louisiana State University, but he has a passionate interest in Confederate history and a driving desire to record that history. With initiative and industry he set himself to write the story of Port Hudson in the war. In the process he unearthed more sources and discovered more information than most people thought existed. He has presented his narrative with verve of style and originality of thought. If sometimes he is inclined to overstate some of the strategic possibilities inherent in the Port Hudson situation, this is the enthusiasm of a budding writer who is not afraid to let his mind play on the "ifs" that are always present in history. His study is a contribution to both Confederate and Civil War literature, and should go far to place Port Hudson and its siege in a proper perspective.

The Louisiana Civil War Centennial Commission has undertaken to underwrite the costs of publication of the book. It has done this because, first, it feels it has an obligation to the people of the South Louisiana area where the battle of Port Hudson was fought to record this memorable experience in print; and because, second and in the larger sense, the commission believes that it can render its greatest and most enduring contribution to Louisiana's Centennial commemoration by publishing books of lasting value.

T. HARRY WILLIAMS
Boyd Professor of History,
Louisiana State University, and
Vice-Chairman,
Louisiana Civil War
Centennial Commission

Acknowledgments

I offer my sincere thanks to all those who gave me assistance and encouragement in the preparation of this work. I especially want to thank Mr. Fred Benton, Jr. and Mr. Charles East of the Committee for the Preservation of the Port Hudson Battlefield for their many kindnesses. To Mr. Benton I owe a debt of gratitude for the photographs used as illustrations in this book. I also want to express my deep appreciation to Mr. Tom Dickey, Atlanta, Georgia, and Miss Frances Otken, McComb, Mississippi, for lending me valuable source materials. Special thanks go to Mr. Ray Smith, Chicago, Illinois, for making available to me his index to the *Confederate Veteran,* and to Mr. V. L. Bedsole, archivist at Louisiana State University, for his cordial assistance. And I am grateful to my mother, Mrs. Hilda Bertus Cunningham, not only for undertaking the job of typing the manuscript but also for the other help, encouragement, and criticism she gave. Finally, to Professor T. Harry Williams, Louisiana State University, who conceived the idea of a study of Port Hudson and who devoted many hours to advising me on both my research and writing—and without whose help this work would never have progressed beyond the first chapter—I sincerely offer my most grateful appreciation.

EDWARD CUNNINGHAM

Table of Contents

Introduction

CONTROL of the Mississippi River, and thus of the Mississippi Valley, was a paramount objective of Union strategy during the great war of 1861–65. In the second year of the war New Orleans, the key to the river, fell. But for the Federals to dominate the lower Mississippi, it was necessary that they capture the Confederate fortified points at Vicksburg, Mississippi, and Port Hudson, Louisiana. And they must capture both, for as long as either held out, the river could not be safely traveled by Union ships.

In early May, 1863, General Ulysses S. Grant commenced operations against Vicksburg, culminating in the great forty-seven-day siege which lasted until July 4 of that year. At approximately the same time, General Nathaniel P. Banks began a series of movements leading to the envelopment of the Confederate garrison at Port Hudson. By May 23 Port Hudson was invested and the small garrison under General Franklin Gardner, consisting of an infantry brigade, a few cavalry, some field batteries, and a small force of heavy artillery, was trapped. In isolating the garrison, Banks committed a serious error, for even as his blue-coated columns surrounded Port Hudson, the Confederate commander received orders to evacuate the post and join with General Joseph E. Johnston's field army in Mississippi. The presence of Banks's army precluded the execution of those orders. By preventing Gardner from pulling his garrison out of Port Hudson, Banks missed an excellent opportunity of destroying the little Confederate army in the open field. Even if he had failed at that, the effect on Union strategy would have still been favorable: Gardner's command could not have added more than five thousand poorly equipped effectives to Johnston's army, and Banks, relieved of the necessity of besieging Port Hudson, could easily have reinforced Grant at Vicksburg with some twenty-odd thousand effectives. As long as the Confederates were at Port Hudson, Banks necessarily had to concentrate virtually the whole of the Nineteenth Army Corps at that point in order to prevent the garrison from sallying out and destroying the besieging force.

Once the siege was joined, the Confederate army was automatically presented with a fantastic collection of tactical and strategical possibilities. The first great possibility was the destruction of Banks's field army. Despite the size of his army, Banks lacked sufficient force to garrison his extended lines. A simultaneous attack by John Logan's cavalry force and Gardner's garrison on the Federal siege lines could have precipitated a disaster, especially after the Union repulse of June 14, 1863. The garrison alone won several opportunities to possibly shatter the besieging force. At any time after 10 A.M. on June 14, a major Confederate counterattack at the "Priest Cap" would have almost certainly broken the siege. Even if Banks had been able to escape south under the protection of the Federal fleet, the blow to Union prestige would have been tremendous, and the way opened for Confederate attacks on Baton Rouge, Donaldsonville, Brashear City, and possibly New Orleans. Any army which had sustained the pounding the Union army took at Port Hudson would have been ineffective as a fighting force for many months. The combined Confederate commands of Logan, Gardner, and Richard Taylor could have badly mauled the Union army, disheartened by its failure before Port Hudson. By using the ravines and gullies running along Confederate Battery No. XI, the Confederates could have broken the backbone of the Federal works and lifted the siege by destroying Banks's heavy guns.

Although the Confederate defense was virtually passive, the siege was nearly lifted by events occurring within the ranks of the Federal army and elsewhere. The tremendous battle casualties, the losses from disease and heat, and the mutiny of certain infantry troops reduced Banks's Army of the Gulf to minimum effectiveness. General Taylor's brilliant campaign in western

Louisiana virtually isolated the army at Port Hudson from the rest of the Federal forces in the state and broke Banks's supply line with New Orleans.

Port Hudson was a campaign of "ifs." If General Kirby Smith had released Taylor for the attack in western Louisiana two weeks earlier; if General Johnston had detached a small force to join with Logan in turning Banks's flanks; if Gardner had counterattacked on June 14; if Banks had lost his nerve in late June or early July when his army began to disintegrate—if any of these had happened, the war in the West could conceivably have taken a radical turn in favor of the Confederacy. The destruction of Banks's army would have meant the recovery of the lower Mississippi Valley by the Confederates. Once Vicksburg fell to Grant, he would undoubtedly have launched an invasion of Louisiana to capture Port Hudson and retake New Orleans. But this would have taken many months and thousands of casualties. There would have been no reinforcements for the Union army in Tennessee, and Grant might not have been there to take command of the army in the dark hours after Chickamauga when the fate of the Union hung in the balance.

The Confederates failed at Port Hudson, but they inflicted such losses on the Army of the Gulf that it never again fought as well as it had before the siege—a disastrous Confederate defeat, but an equally disastrous Union victory.

THE PORT HUDSON CAMPAIGN

I

Prelude

IN the spring of 1862 the Civil War entered its second year with the military situation thoroughly confused and generally unfavorable to the Confederacy. By pressing their plan of securing Southern seaports, Federal forces had, in the first twelve months of fighting, virtually succeeded in isolating the eastern Confederacy from Europe. It became increasingly difficult to bring in the munitions of war manufactured by Britain, France, Belgium and The Netherlands which the South needed in order to survive. War matériel could be brought in through the seaports on the Gulf of Mexico, but it was not easy to transport equipment and supplies to the main Confederate field armies in Virginia and Tennessee. The Federals soon sought to cut off even this supply route by attacking the ports along the Gulf. Blockading squadrons closed off partially or completely Mobile, Biloxi, Galveston, and New Orleans.

From the first few weeks of the war, it was obvious that the great theaters of operation were to be along the lines of the Potomac, Cumberland, and Tennessee rivers. Along these waterways, which provided means of transportation and communication, the armies of Meade, Hooker, Buell, Thomas, Rosecrans, Grant, Burnside, Bragg, McClellan, Johnston, and Lee would fight it out to decide the destiny of the North American continent. The territory across the Mississippi River took on added importance, for munitions could be brought to Mexico, a neutral country, and then shipped across the Rio Grande to the hard-pressed Confederate armies.

Possession of the Mississippi became more and more important to the Federals as a means of cutting off supplies from the

Confederate armies fighting east of the river. There were also political and economic reasons why the Union would like to isolate the two segments of the Southern Confederacy. Military victories in this theater would provide a cheap source of morale, and the conquered lands of Louisiana, Mississippi, Texas, and Arkansas could produce cotton to feed the New England textile mills. The Federals needed the Mississippi River, and early in the war determined to take it no matter what the price.

In the beginning New Orleans was the key to the river, hence possibly to the entire Confederacy. As long as the city held out, blockade-runners could slip past patrolling Yankee ships at the mouths of the Mississippi and steam upriver to disgorge their valuable cargoes. New Orleans, the largest city in the Confederacy, was the economic center of the Southwest, possessing the only banking system that might be used to finance the Confederate war effort. Warships and various other military equipment could be produced in the city, and it was a fertile ground for recruiting troops.

New Orleans, then, must be taken. However, Federal military heads realized that an assault was a risky proposition. The prelude to the attack was the occupation of Ship Island on September 17, 1861, by the West Gulf Blockading Squadron. This island off the Mississippi coast was of value as an advanced staging area and supply base because of its proximity to the mouths of the Mississippi River. The Gulf campaign took an important turn when David G. Farragut was formally appointed to command the squadron on January 9, 1862. In February of that year Flag Officer Farragut arrived at Ship Island to plan the actual operation of taking New Orleans. It was late March before the campaign began, and even then it was nearly a month before Farragut could get his heavy ships over the shallow sand bars and in position to attack Forts Jackson and St. Philip, which guarded the river below New Orleans. After a five-day bombardment, Farragut's warships ran the forts and attacked the tiny Confederate fleet, smashing it to pieces within minutes. Isolated, the forts surrendered, and on May 1 General Benjamin F. Butler occupied New Orleans.[1]

The fall of the city was a hard blow to the cause of Southern independence. Farragut's victorious squadron steamed up the undefended river, capturing Baton Rouge and Natchez. The lower Mississippi was now open to Federal conquest; the situation on the upper Mississippi was equally desperate.

New Madrid, Island No. 10, Memphis, and Fort Pillow soon fell before the hard-driving Federal ironclads and their army supports. Only Vicksburg remained in the hands of the Confederacy, and a bold thrust might have secured it for the Union. The Confederates erected a few batteries on the bluffs above the river and prepared to defend the city to the last man. On June 26, 1862, the combined upper and lower Mississippi squadrons commenced operations against the weak Confederate defenses, but the naval bombardment was a failure.

At Yazoo City, Mississippi, Lieutenant Isaac N. Brown of the Confederate Navy succeeded in getting the ram *Arkansas* into fighting shape, and on July 14, 1862, he steamed down to meet the Union fleet at Vicksburg. After some of the most desperate fighting of the war, the crew of this little ironclad and the Confederate gunners of the Vicksburg batteries forced the Federals to abandon the assault.

Early the following month Confederate forces under General John C. Breckinridge attacked Union-held Baton Rouge. The assault failed when the *Arkansas,* steaming south to support Breckinridge, broke down within sight of her goal and had to be blown up by her own crew.

But the attack convinced Butler that Baton Rouge was too exposed a position, and two weeks later he ordered the evacuation of the city.

The scene of war on the Mississippi was about to undergo a rapid change as a new position of military importance came into play. After their failure to retake Baton Rouge, the Confederates faced the difficult problem of securing the southern flank of their base at Vicksburg from the possibility of an attack up the river. To guard this last major bastion on the Mississippi, the Confederate high command proposed to establish a fortified position at a place suitable for strong defense. The logical position was Port

Hudson, Louisiana. No other place on the river, except Vicksburg, was better adapted for the purpose.[2]

Located twenty-five miles upriver from Baton Rouge, about a hundred and fifty miles by river from New Orleans, and a hundred and ten miles downriver from Vicksburg, Port Hudson barred "the ascent of the river as Vicksburg did the descent."[3] Moreover, it was forty miles below the mouth of the Red River, and could command the southern approaches to that vital avenue of supply.

The little town on the east bank of the Mississippi was situated on an "almost precipitous bluff" just where the river made a sharp turn to the south.[4] It overlooked a wide stretch of alluvial plain on the opposite shore. At the bottom of the bluff was a narrow bank upon which grew willows, cottonwoods, and other saplings. During high water this strip was often flooded. Here the river was slowly making deposits of alluvium, which had the effect of changing its course, and this in turn cut away at the peninsula in the southwestern crook of the bend. The channel of the river was such that vessels rounding the bend kept close to the east bank—and the towering Port Hudson bluff. This natural stronghold, with its lofty rises, was several miles long and varied in height from sixty to eighty feet.

The countryside in and around Port Hudson was broken by embankments, hollows, and ravines, many of them deep enough to obstruct the movement of men and horses. Roads ran to Clinton, Jackson, Bayou Sara, and to Mississippi northward; to Ross's Landing, Springfield Landing, and Baton Rouge southward; to both the Comite and Amite rivers eastward. Port Hudson was the terminus of the Clinton and Port Hudson Railroad, twenty-one miles in length when finally completed. This line connected the two small communities for the prosperity of both.

Some 30,000 bales of cotton and 2,000 hogsheads of sugar were shipped from the Port annually.[5] Even after the beginning of hostilities, the town carried on a considerable commerce. Salt was vitally needed by the Confederacy, and the lack of it seriously hurt the provisioning of the Confederate armies. Salt was brought in from St. Mary Parish and ferried over the river on

THE LOWER MISSISSIPPI

flats. It was then shipped on the Clinton railroad and hauled by oxen to Jackson, Mississippi, to a railroad there.[6] Sugar, tobacco, and other items were shipped in the same manner. The landing place known as Hickey's, at the foot of the Port Hudson bluff, was a difficult one because of the strong eddies and high banks.[7] The formation of a sand bar there hurt commerce considerably, and by 1864 the landing was completely unusable.[8]

The town of Port Hudson consisted of "densely crowded rows of handsome and costly warehouses, stores, saloons, and hotels, between which and the steamboats a long line of loaded country wagons plied almost incessantly."[9] Buildings of frame construction included several general mercantile stores, drug-stores, a lodge building, and a turntable on the railroad.[10] There were about twelve or fifteen stores in the town before the fighting began.[11] There were twenty-eight streets, but apparently many were never graded. There were probably close to fifty houses in the town proper, and a number of plantations, both large and small, scattered around the outskirts of the town. A community of this size must have had a full complement of blacksmith shops, livery stables, and the like. A cemetery was located just north of the northwest corner of the town limits.

Port Hudson was, on the eve of the war, a typical small Southern town, peaceful and not stirring with ambition for the future. Its citizens could have had no knowledge that their home was to become the center of one of the crucial campaigns of the conflict in which the North and South were soon to be engaged.

II

River Bastion

EVEN before the fall of New Orleans the Confederates were paying some attention to Port Hudson. About the first of April, 1862, minor earthworks were erected on the bluffs above the town. These earthworks were "but a mere wall with a dry ditch, from which the earth had been cast to make a wall about four and a half feet high, and not over five or six feet broad at the top; the base from eight to fifteen feet thick." [1] The line of works started near Sandy Creek on the Mississippi River and "ran back for a quarter of a mile, and thence forming a section of a circle, it extended southward for about three quarters of a mile and then turned back toward the river, which it reached about a mile and a quarter below the place of starting." [2] These works were probably finished after the fall of New Orleans, but were apparently not garrisoned by the Confederates. Southern authorities failed to perceive the value of Port Hudson until the middle of the summer of 1862.

In late July, 1862, General Earl Van Dorn directed General Breckinridge to attack Union forces holding Baton Rouge and to secure and fortify Port Hudson.[3] On August 5 Breckinridge launched his gallant but unsuccessful attack on Louisiana's occupied capital. He then withdrew his small command a short distance from the city, and a few days later sent troops to occupy Port Hudson. The actual occupation took place on the evening of August 15, as Colonel R. P. Trabue moved into the Port with the advance guard, consisting of his regiment and part of Robert Cobb's battery. On the following day more Confederate troops and equipment, under Brigadier General Daniel Ruggles, arrived.

9

General Ruggles' orders were to fortify Port Hudson, using any means feasible. Supplies would be sent to him from Clinton by railroad, and Ruggles was directed to accumulate as large a quantity of provisions as possible. He was given authority to obtain entrenching tools and labor, and he was specifically directed to guard and control the approaches to Baton Rouge.[4]

Confederate authorities were beginning to appreciate the strategic importance of Port Hudson, and provisions were made to send matériel and men to reinforce the garrison. Secretary of War George W. Randolph suggested to General Robert E. Lee that Lieutenant Colonel Paul Francis De Gournay's battalion, which comprised part of the Richmond garrison, be sent to Port Hudson to act as heavy artillerymen.[5] De Gournay, a Frenchman of noble birth and an ardent Confederate, had won an enviable reputation as an artillerist in the fighting along the Peninsula. His battalion, which arrived at Port Hudson in late August, 1862, was destined to play a major role in the defense of the bastion.[6]

Major General Richard Taylor immediately established communications with General Ruggles, and if possible, was to send the general some heavy artillery.[7] Soon after Ruggles commenced fortifying Port Hudson, Breckinridge arrived to make an informal inspection. The general found that under the able direction of Captain James Nocquet the earthworks were rapidly taking shape, that some of them were even ready to take the heavy guns which were reportedly on the way. Breckinridge was ordered to Jackson, Mississippi, with the bulk of his command, thus leaving Ruggles with but a small force to defend the newly acquired position.[8]

The evacuation of Baton Rouge by the Federals on August 21, 1862, removed the immediate possibility of a Federal land advance on Port Hudson. Ruggles was soon to follow Breckinridge northward, being ordered to relinquish his command to General W. N. R. Beall. This change of command took place on August 29.[9] Five days before, the Union ironclad *Essex* proceeded on a patrol up the Mississippi to reconnoiter the batteries reported to be under construction at Port Hudson. The

Federals could see no evidence of artillery, but reported that earthworks were being built.[10] Commodore W. D. Porter ordered his gunners to open fire on them. Because of the bursting of a 10-inch gun aboard the *Essex,* the fire was largely ineffectual. Apparently there were no casualties.

On August 29 the Union steamer *Anglo-American* attempted to pass Port Hudson, and her captain, P. K. Riley, noticed that earthworks had been erected on the bluff and along the water line. Failing to observe any cannon, Riley continued steaming up the Mississippi for about a mile, when he discovered a fortified Confederate position. The Federals opened fire with a 50-pound rifle, but because of wet powder their shooting was not effective. Crouched behind their earthworks, Confederate gunners calculated the proper aim, loaded their pieces, and started blasting. Chaos broke loose when the sharp-eyed Southerners scored seventy-three hits on the hapless Federal steamer. The captain of the *Anglo-American* decided to effect an immediate withdrawal. Despite the accuracy of the Confederate fire, only two Federal sailors were wounded. Riley reported that he had been under fire from two 32-pounders and eighteen field pieces of 6 and 12-pound caliber.[11] Oddly enough, the Confederate gunners believed they had struck the *Anglo-American* only four or five times, and they were annoyed by their failure to sink the Union ship.

On the seventh of the following month the Confederate gunners got another chance at the *Anglo-American,* as well as their old foe the *Essex.* At 4:15 A.M. the two ships attempted to slip past and ran into a hot fire from the batteries. The Confederates pounded the ships with two 42-pounders, a 20-pounder, and several field pieces. The *Essex* returned the fire, hitting one Confederate horse and killing it. Commodore Porter reported that he had "reason to believe the enemy was considerably damaged." [12] Young Sarah Morgan, a refugee from Baton Rouge who was staying with relatives nearby, made light of the Yankee side of the story in her diary: "The Captain reports having been fired on by a battery of thirty-six large guns, at Port Hudson

. . . when he opened fire and silenced them, one after the other, from the first to the last." [13] The losses of the Confederates "must have been awful," she wrote facetiously.

The *Essex* was struck fourteen times, but damage was slight; the Confederate projectiles were too light to penetrate the ship's armor. Because the *Anglo-American* ran past while stationed on the starboard side of the ironclad, she escaped damage from the Confederate fire.

To garrison and defend their new post, the Confederates needed men, guns, and supplies, and the task of obtaining these fell heavily on the shoulders of General Ruggles and his successor, General Beall. Before the passage of the *Essex,* heavy guns could be brought to Port Hudson only "by hauling the guns over the steep hills and miserable roads that led through the piney woods between Jackson [Mississippi] railroad and the Mississippi." [14] Some of the cannon brought to Port Hudson already had a colorful history, having been captured by Virginia authorities when they seized the Norfolk Navy Yard on April 20, 1861. [15]

Despite the difficulty in procuring guns, the Confederates persevered, and by October 24, 1862, had accumulated quite an assortment of cannon. Their biggest weapon was a 10-inch Columbiad gun mounted in Battery No. V. There were only ninety-nine rounds of shot and shell available for this weapon, however; hence its value was somewhat limited. The Confederates had a single 8-inch Columbiad located in Battery No. IV, which was well supplied with ammunition, including grapeshot. Together with the 42-pounder located in Battery No. I, the two Columbiads constituted the only guns Port Hudson possessed strong enough to hurt the Federal ironclads. There were three 32-pound rifled barbette guns located in Battery No. III (the water battery), but at the time only one of these was mounted, and the ammunition supply was limited, comprising only fifty rounds of shell and a hundred and thirty of shot. Batteries No. II, VIII, X, and XI were provided with a total of ten 24-pound rifled guns, only four of these being mounted on siege carriages. These weapons were provided with solid shot, shell, spherical case shot, grape, and canister, and there was a good supply of cartridges on hand. There were fourteen guns actually mounted and ready for use.[16]

Confederate engineers had constructed magazines for the various batteries, but most of these were improperly placed, being exposed to potential fire from the river. The main magazine was located about a half mile inland in a growth of wood. The position was considered safe, and the magazine was covered with four feet of timber and nine feet of earth. To bolster the river batteries, the Confederates had four light or field batteries, under Captains R. M. Boone, C. Roberts, C. E. Fenner, and J. L. Bradford. The four batteries counted twenty-two field pieces, of which six were fairly modern 12-pound bronze howitzers. The remainder were obsolescent 6-pound guns.[17]

As of August 31, 1862, the Port Hudson garrison consisted of the Thirtieth Louisiana Infantry Regiment, Miles' Louisiana Legion, Captain C. McLaurin's partisan ranger company, plus the artillery companies. The total number of men was 946, of whom 404 were artillerymen and 97 were cavalry.[18] This was a small force with which to hold such an important point, but there were other troops in the area which could be brought in to reinforce the Port in case of need.

Beall's report of October 22, 1862, indicates that his command, including the garrisons at Baton Rouge, Covington, Ponchatoula, and Camp Moore, numbered 3,385 men.[19] Although Beall lacked troops, the situation was partly remedied when reinforcements were moved down from Jackson, Mississippi. General John B. Villepigue was ordered to proceed to Port Hudson on October 24.[20] His seasoned brigade, veterans of the battle of Corinth, immediately followed him, arriving at Port Hudson on November 5. Unfortunately for the cause of the Confederacy, Villepigue, a brave and competent officer, died November 9, 1862, of cholera morbus.[21]

Life at Port Hudson was fairly quiet and routine. Each morning at daybreak there was reveille, followed by roll call. Then the Confederate soldiers went through the "delightful" procedure of inspection of arms and policing the camp. At six o'clock they held drill; at seven there was breakfast. The soldiers then engaged in guard mounting, while the non-commissioned officers drilled. At ten the companies would fall out, and there was more drill. At twelve o'clock noon came dinner, followed at three by dress parade. Apparently the members of the garrison were allowed a few hours on their own after sunset and retreat, but lights-out came at 9 P.M.[22] For these hardy veterans of Corinth, Island No. 10, Shiloh, and Fort Donelson, this was a mild regime. The food was fairly good; there were abundant rations of beef, sugar, salt, corn meal, and molasses. Occasionally potatoes were issued to the messes, and those soldiers who had a few dollars could buy extras from the surrounding farms and stores. Pumpkins were plentiful on the plantations around Port Hudson, and often the men dined on pumpkin pie.[23]

The river and the local cypress ponds furnished Louisiana catfish. But the water was not fit to drink. "That taken from the river, if left to stand for a few days, became measurably clear by the settling of the mud." [24] Some of the men managed to find barrels, and with molasses and corn made a type of beer which was very palatable. They did a thriving business with this beverage. Another delicacy which also found a ready sale was made from flour and mashed sweet potatoes. The men baked this mixture into round cakes and called it sweet potato pone. Several men from the Forty-ninth Tennessee were so actively engaged in this industry, as they peddled "their pones through the camp," that the French-speaking Thirtieth Louisiana Regiment would shout as they went out to drill: "Here comes your sweet 'tater pones." [25]

Each mess detailed some of its members or hired Negro cooks to take care of the actual food preparation. The women of the community frequently aided the soldiers, some of whom had trouble even boiling water. Some of the canny Alabamans built an oven eighteen inches in diameter and five inches deep, in which they boiled rice. By adding sugar and spices they made forty-pound "globs" of rice pudding.[26]

Reverend J. H. McNeilly of the Forty-ninth Tennessee never forgot the beef served to the men in camp. After the war he wrote: "But the memory of the beef that was served to us for a good while is still nauseating. Poor, gristly blue, gummy, it could be boiled for hours and never an eye of grease on the water." [27]

At least some of the Confederates had tents, a few of which probably had been captured from the Federals in past actions. As winter approached, permanent barracks were constructed to house the troops. The cabins were made of willow logs and "were 18 by 22 feet, with a large fireplace at each end. The chimneys were built of sticks daubed with clay. An open doorway furnished entrance and light, while ventilation was secured by leaving the upper cracks between the logs unchinked." [28] Bunks were built along the walls in tiers. The Confederate soldiers were cheerful, spending their off-duty time in the traditional way of all soldiers, flirting with the local belles and getting into mischief. Many lacked shoes, jackets, and shirts. Young Sarah Morgan described them thus:

Men who had fought at Shiloh and Baton Rouge were barefooted. Rags was their only uniform, for very few possessed a complete suit, and those few wore all varieties of colors and cuts. Hats could be seen of every style and shape, from the first ever invented down to the last one purchased evidently some time since. Yet he who had no shoes looked as happy as he who had, and he who had a cap had something to toss up, that's all.[29]

Undaunted by their motley look, they continued to train for the time when they would meet the enemy. The quiet and somewhat dull days at Port Hudson were about to end. The Union command was preparing to strike. On Sunday, November 16, 1862, the Federal fleet boldly steamed up and commenced a brief bombardment of the Confederate batteries. The Confederates deployed sharpshooters along the river, but they were unable to bring the Yankee warships into action, and the Federals soon withdrew, pausing only to fire at a few sugar houses.[30] The action was bloodless, and for almost a month things were quiet. However, on December 13 the U.S.S. *Winona* and the *Essex* anchored off the upper end of Profit Island. The Confederates immediately determined to drive them away.

Boone's light artillery company and Companies D and F of the First Alabama crossed the Mississippi on the evening of December 13 and made their way downriver to a point opposite the anchorage of the Union ships. The Confederate gunners planted their weapons, two smoothbore 6-pounders and a 12-pound howitzer, behind the levee. At dawn the next morning the Yankee ships found themselves under heavy fire, which they immediately returned, blazing away with grape, canister, and shrapnel. The Federal gunners were unable to elevate their weapons to bear on the Confederate guns and were thus unable to silence them. The Confederate fire was so deadly that the *Essex* had to steam over and interpose her iron sides to protect the wooden *Winona*. The *Winona* ran aground, complicating matters further, but succeeded in getting off. Confederate soldiers opened fire on her with their muskets. The fire from the batteries was more effective, severely damaging the *Winona* and killing one man. The Union ships withdrew down the river.[31]

The period of long-range Union naval patrols was about to end as operations entered a more serious phase. On December 17, 1862, the Federals reoccupied Baton Rouge, which they had abandoned the previous August. The play war on the lower Mississippi was about to end.

III

The Campaign Begins

EVEN while the Confederate garrison at Port Hudson prepared for the winter, events were taking place in New Orleans which would have a marked effect on the outcome of the war in the Mississippi Valley. General Butler had attracted great notoriety by his methods of ruling occupied Louisiana, and late in 1862 the administration in Washington replaced Butler with General Nathaniel P. Banks, who arrived in New Orleans with strong reinforcements. Banks, one of the so-called political generals, was aggressive in battle, but he was a poor handler of troops. In his previous service in Virginia he had suffered several reverses, although the faults he would later display were not at this time clearly apparent. Despite his military ineptitude, Banks, a former Democrat and now a prominent Republican, had to be treated with consideration. The "Bobbin Boy's" [1] position was slightly shaky as the radicals in Washington attempted to get their good friend Butler reinstated. Pressure was brought to bear on the President to oust Banks and send him on an expedition to Texas, but Lincoln finally decided to maintain the status quo in Louisiana and employ Butler in some other capacity. [2]

The actual change of command took place on December 15, 1862, Banks having arrived by steamer at New Orleans the day before. He brought with him a force of thirty-nine infantry regiments, six field batteries, and one cavalry battalion. Twenty-two of the infantry regiments were nine-month troops. [3] On the following day Banks sent General Cuvier Grover with twelve infantry regiments, three field batteries, and two cavalry troops up the Mississippi River to capture Baton Rouge. The small Con-

17

federate garrison withdrew without a fight, leaving the city to the invaders.

General Beall had only about 5,500 men at Port Hudson at this time,[4] and it is possible that if Banks had brought his main force up the river and attacked from the landward side, he might well have won a notable victory. In early January, Banks was ordered to commence operations of some sort in the Port Hudson area in order to relieve the pressure on General Ulysses S. Grant, who was at Vicksburg. Banks failed to make any movement, however, and Grant determined to send part of Porter's fleet to run the Vicksburg batteries, disrupt transportation on the Red River, and isolate Port Hudson from Vicksburg by the water route.

Colonel Charles R. Ellet, captain of the ram *Queen of the West*, ran the batteries the morning of February 3, 1863, passed down the river by Natchez, and proceeded up the Red River, destroying several Confederate steamers carrying supplies and passengers. Among the ships destroyed were the *Moro* and the *Berwick Bay*, loaded with several weeks' rations for Port Hudson. The *Queen of the West* was finally captured by the Confederates at Gordon's Landing, Louisiana, although Ellet and most of his men escaped on the captured steamer *Grand Era*.

At Fort DeRussey, Major Joseph L. Brent collected a force to attack the *Indianola*, consisting of the captured *Queen of the West*, the little steamer *Webb*, and the tender *Era No. V*. Brent's squadron entered the Mississippi River on February 22. There it was joined by the *Dr. Beatty*, an old cattle boat armed with a 20-pound Parrott and carrying two hundred volunteers from the Port Hudson garrison.[5] Brent's squadron caught up with the *Indianola* near New Carthage, Louisiana, on the night of February 24 and captured her after a lengthy and desperate battle. The men on the *Dr. Beatty* assisted in the capture by raking the Union ship with blasts of rifle fire and finally boarded her to accept the captain's surrender. The sailors from the two captured Union ships were taken to Vicksburg, but were removed to Richmond when the siege began.[6] By capturing the *Queen of the West* and the *Indianola*, the Confederates regained control of the Red

River and that part of the Mississippi between Vicksburg and Port Hudson.[7]

Their period of control was brief, for even at that time Banks and Farragut were planning an offensive operation against Port Hudson. Banks was to make a demonstration against the Port while the fleet ran past. There was no idea of a grand assault on the bastion, for the Confederate army was considered too strong to be defeated. It was seriously thought by some of Banks's officers that the Port would fall if Farragut succeeded in blockading the Red River.[8]

By March 7, 1863, Banks had assembled a marching force of three divisions—those of Christopher C. Augur, William Emory, and Cuvier Grover—at Baton Rouge, totaling more than 15,000 men. To protect his flanks, Banks left General T. W. Sherman to cover New Orleans and General Godfrey Weitzel to hold LaFourche. On March 9 Banks's command prepared to march on Port Hudson. But not all of Farragut's fleet had arrived. Not until March 12 were the warships assembled at Baton Rouge, and Banks celebrated the occasion with a grand review of his army on the battlefield of August 5. The review was impressive and Banks glowed with confidence. The Union army and navy were ready to strike at Port Hudson, with only the final orders to be given.[9]

While Union Louisiana was undergoing the change in administration from Butler to Banks, things had also been happening at the Confederate bastion at Port Hudson. On December 27, 1862, Major General Franklin Gardner quietly stepped off a car of the Clinton and Port Hudson Railroad and presented himself at garrison headquarters. There were no formal celebrations or ceremonies as Gardner unobtrusively inspected Port Hudson with General Beall and his staff. On the succeeding day, December 28, Beall formally relinquished his command to the West Point-trained and New York-born Confederate.[10]

The members of the garrison were favorably impressed by Gardner. A highly competent engineer, he immediately set out to alter the system of river defense, clustering the heaviest guns together so as to deliver a more concentrated fire on any passing ship. And he began to revamp the entire Port Hudson defensive network, including the earthworks.[11]

Prior to Gardner's arrival, three different plans of defense had been considered. The first plan, which was really never started, was that of a classical style fortress along the lines laid down by the French marshal Vauban. This plan would have required a garrison much smaller in size than any of the others, and would have presented a more concentrated and effective fire; however, it would have enabled forces attacking by both land and water to rain so heavy a destructive fire on so small an area as to make it untenable without the usual casements of a regularly constructed fort of stone. The second plan was a series of open lunettes—simple earthworks in the form of a V, each flanking the other at a distance of four hundred yards. The third and last plan was an ordinary indented line—parapet and ditch.

The second plan had been selected, and work on it had begun. The first lunette was built on the Baton Rouge road, four miles away from Port Hudson. The plan called for the building of a line of lunettes from the river below to a certain point on Sandy Creek. Seven of these lunettes were constructed immediately, commanding the Baton Rouge road, and the others were on the various fields through which the line of defense was to run. The entire line would have been eight miles in length, and according to military rule would have had to have a force of 28,000 men and a reserve of 7,000 men, with some seventy pieces of artillery. This plan was shortly abandoned, being considered impracticable. General Beall actually deserves considerable credit for the plan of defense next adopted. Work was immediately begun on this plan as described by Lieutenant Howard Wright:

A line was surveyed, commencing about two miles and a half below Port Hudson, describing a slight curve to a point on Sandy creek, a mile back of the town. For about three-quarters of a mile from the river the line crossed a broken series of ridges, plateaus and ravines, taking advantage of high ground in some places and in others extending down a steep declivity; for the next mile and a quarter it traversed Gibbon's and Slaughter's fields where a wide level plain seemed formed on purpose for a battlefield; another quarter of a mile carried it through fields and over hills to a deep gorge, in the bosom of which lay Sandy creek. From thence to the river was about a mile and a half. This was a line four miles and a half long.[12]

The Confederates at Port Hudson, like their brethren in Virginia and the Carolinas, had no great enthusiasm for hard work; consequently, slave labor was used in erecting most of the fortifications. But as the situation became more serious, they overcame their scruples against work and enthusiastically applied themselves with picks and shovels.

The number of troops at Port Hudson was constantly increased as a means of offsetting the threat of Banks and his army. By March, Gardner had organized his garrison into four brigades under the command of Generals W. N. R. Beall, S. B. Maxey, John Gregg, and Albert Rust. Provisioning such a large force put a severe strain on the Confederate commissary. The natural difficulties of obtaining supplies were further complicated by constant bungling and mismanagement.[13]

The raids of the *Queen of the West* and the *Indianola* also handicapped the gathering of provisions, and even for the sparse quantities of supplies collected, there was a lack of adequate storage space at Port Hudson. It was remarked many times by officers of high grade and military ability that "if Port Hudson falls, we will have to thank the commissary department for it." [14] The department was not well organized from the very beginning, and though there was some effort put forth to try and improve matters, nothing concrete was accomplished.

The Confederate situation at Port Hudson was reasonably secure in early March, 1863, despite the difficulties of supply, and the Confederate troops were ready to fight the Northern invader.[15] Their opportunity was about to arrive. The campaign opened with a Federal raid on the Comite River bridges in an attempt to interrupt Confederate communications. The raiding party consisted of Colonel T. E. Chickering's Forty-first Massachusetts Infantry, one cavalry company, and two cannon from Ormand F. Nims's Massachusetts battery. Leaving Baton Rouge, the Union force split into two groups, the smaller of which burned Bogler's Bridge but was repulsed in an attempt to burn Strickland's Bridge. Chickering reunited his two groups and launched a heavy assault on the Confederate garrison at Strickland's Bridge, driving the outnumbered Southerners away after a sharp engagement. The bridge was burned and Chickering's command returned to Baton Rouge without further incident.[16]

While Banks in Baton Rouge was holding his grand review on March 12, troops from the Fifty-third Massachusetts Infantry conducted a reconnaissance in the direction of Port Hudson. Two steamers, escorted by the *Albatross,* landed the troops on the east bank of the Mississippi about five miles north of Baton Rouge. Escorted by eighteen cavalrymen, the men of the Fifty-third advanced overland to the Bayou Sara Road, where they drove in Confederate pickets. After capturing some cattle, they returned to Baton Rouge.[17]

Finally, Banks commenced his forward movement, sending General Grover and his division northward on the evening of March 13, with General Emory and his division following the next morning and General Christopher Augur covering the rear. About 2 P.M. on March 14 the Federal signal officers opened communications with Farragut's naval force, which was anchored near Profit Island. Banks deployed troops to protect the avenue of communication. About 5 P.M. the fleet signaled that Farragut had decided to make the passage of the Port Hudson batteries at 8 P.M. instead of the following morning.[18]

The sudden change of time threw Banks off balance momentarily. His troops were still several miles from Port Hudson, and by nightfall were not in position to aid in the passage of the fleet by creating a diversionary action in the rear as had been originally planned. Admiral Farragut and his sailors were going to be on their own. This would be a navy show.

IV

March 14

PREPARATIONS for the passage of the Port Hudson batteries by Farragut's fleet began in early March, 1863, as the *Hartford*, the *Monongahela*, and the *Richmond* arrived at Baton Rouge to join the *Essex*,[1] the *Mississippi*, and the other gunboats and mortar schooners already assembled there. Farragut's striking force was a powerful one. The *Hartford* and the *Richmond*, commanded respectively by Captains James S. Palmer and James Alden, were screw sloops, mounting 9-inch Dahlgrens in their broadside batteries and rifled pivot guns. The *Mississippi*, a side-wheeler which had carried Commodore Matthew C. Perry to Japan in 1854, carried a main battery of 8-inch Dahlgrens, plus a 10-inch pivot gun and several smaller weapons. Captain Melancton Smith commanded her. The *Monongahela*, commanded by Captain J. B. McKinstry, was a second-class screw sloop, mounting fourteen guns. Farragut's only armored ship, the *Essex*, mounting six heavy guns, was commanded by Charles Henry Caldwell. Because of her poor engines, Farragut decided not to use her in the actual attack. His secondary battle line consisted of the gunboats *Kineo, Albatross, Genesee,* and *Sachem*, plus six mortar schooners armed with 13-inch mortars, against which the Port Hudson Confederates had no defense.[2]

The United States Navy was well represented in fighting strength on the lower Mississippi. To improve the performance of these fighting ships, there was a minute inspection of each vessel. And there was great activity on board the Federal warships in preparation for battle.

Running rigging was taken down, splinter nettings were placed on the starboard side, and everything put in readiness for the engagement. Barricades were placed around the steam and engine room bulkheads, and bulwarks of hammocks were made around the top forecastle.[3]

To increase her efficiency, Farragut's flagship, the U.S.S. *Hartford,* was provided with a speaking tube running from her mizzenmast to the wheel. The pilot, Thomas R. Carroll, was placed in the mizzenmast where he could direct the ship's movements effectively.[4]

It was Farragut's belief that the passage of the river batteries at Port Hudson was a matter of the utmost importance. Since the beginning of the year it had been his intention to pass the Port, but Confederate operations at Mobile, Galveston, and Sabine Pass had delayed his executing the operation. When he received the news that the *Indianola* had been lost, he decided upon action. "The time has come, there can be no delay," Farragut told Captain T. A. Jenkins, his chief of staff. "I must go, army or no army." [5] He thus expressed the importance of what he had to do:

The first object to be accomplished is to cripple the Southern armies by cutting off their supplies from Texas. Texas at this time is, and must continue to be to the end of the war their main dependence for beef cattle, sheep, and Indian corn. If we can get a few vessels above Port Hudson the thing will not be an entire failure, and I am pretty confident it can be done.[6]

Farragut's main objective was to pass the Port with the least possible damage to his ships so that they could immediately continue operations up both the Mississippi and Red rivers. He wanted to knock out the formidable Confederate obstruction that had been prepared by the Rebels, and he was anxious to get started. The plan, agreed upon with Banks, was that the army would create a diversionary action in the rear of Port Hudson so as to draw off field batteries from the bluffs.[7]

Before undertaking the operation, Farragut made extensive preparations in order to insure the success of the expedition. To give the *Hartford, Richmond, Monongahela,* and *Mississippi* some protection from Confederate fire, chain cables were arranged on the starboard side of each vessel.[8] These iron cables were also expected to keep off the "cottonclad" steamers, which the Confederates were known to be using as rams. Some cables were also arranged vertically on the ships' starboard sides to protect the vulnerable boilers from a chance enemy projectile.[9] The maintop and foretop of the *Hartford* were rimmed with boiler iron to protect the men who would be stationed there from enemy fire.

Farragut decided upon a novel experiment in arranging his warships for the passage. The weak gunboats were lashed to the sides of the sturdier screw sloops. In the event one ship was disabled, her partner could tow her, and the maneuverability of both would be increased—a significant fact in view of the bend in the river just beyond the main Port Hudson batteries.

On the afternoon of March 13, 1863, the *Essex* and the mortar schooners appeared near the head of Profit Island, where they anchored.[10] Farragut, with the rest of his powerful naval force, soon followed, and when the fog lifted on the following morning the entire Federal fleet lay at anchor just out of range of the Confederate cannon. Farragut called for one last meeting of his commanders to discuss the forthcoming battle. All possibilities were considered, and the Federals completed their final plans and preparations.[11]

The admiral instructed his captains to keep their positions during the passage so that they would not become confused and fire into each other. Any ship passing Port Hudson was to proceed to the mouth of the Red River and harass Confederate river transportation. Farragut's last order was that the best protection from Confederate fire was a "well-directed fire from our own guns, shell and shrapnel at a distance and grape when within four hundred or five hundred yards." [12]

During the afternoon of March 14 the Federal warships commenced a brief bombardment of Port Hudson, firing perhaps seventy-five projectiles in order to establish the exact ranges of the Confederate batteries. The Confederates were thoroughly alerted and prepared for a fight.

Instead of waiting for the following dawn, as had been agreed with Banks, Farragut decided to launch his attack before mid-night. Communications were established with Banks's headquarters, notifying him that the time of attack had been advanced.[13] About 9 P.M., March 14, 1863, the signal to weigh anchor was given. The order was not instantly obeyed, and it was well past ten o'clock before the fleet was in motion.[14]

Admiral Farragut, on the *Hartford,* led the way, with the *Albatross* lashed to her. The *Richmond,* with the *Genesee* fastened to her, was second in the column of attack. The *Monongahela,* fastened to the *Kineo* with hawsers, was third, and the *Mississippi,* which was not lashed to a gunboat because of her paddle wheels, brought up the rear.[15] The current against the advancing ships was nearly five knots, so the eight-knot vessels could only move upstream at a speed comparable to a normal man's walk.[16] To take the 90-degree turn under the Confederate guns, Farragut counted on the double leverage accruing from the lashing together of the ships.

As the seven ships approached, Captain J. W. Youngblood of the Confederate Signal Corps, stationed on the east bank opposite Troth's Landing, ignited a signal rocket to warn the Confederate gunners of the attack. Sentinels fired their muskets into the air, and the Confederates dashed to man their guns.[17]

Realizing that their approach had been discovered, the Federals launched two signal rockets from the deck of the *Hartford* as a signal for the *Essex,* the *Sachem,* and the mortar flotilla, which had remained behind at anchorage below Troth's Landing, to open fire. The rest of the fleet soon joined in the fire, but the Confederate guns remained silent. Colonel De Gournay fired the first gun [18] as the *Hartford* was nearly opposite Battery No. XI. To illuminate the enemy ships, the Confederates ignited great bonfires under the bluff, but the smoke from the pine wood only served to further confuse the Confederate gunners, and the fires were quickly put out.[19] The advancing ships were forced to hug the water near the eastern bluff in order to avoid the shoals that jutted out from the west bank. The noise and confusion reached thunderous proportions as more than a hundred cannon roared.

Leading the attack, the *Hartford* was in by far the best position, as she did not have smoke from any other ship clouding her visibility. Visibility was still poor, however, because of the unusual atmospheric conditions, the Confederate bonfires, and the smoke from the cannon. The flagship moved steadily ahead. She was hulled several times, and was somewhat cut up in the rigging, but the damage was not serious.[20] Only one incident disturbed the even tempo of the well handled warship. A lookout yelled, "Ram on the port bow, Sir!" Palmer ordered, "Man the port battery and call away the boarders." Farragut grabbed his cutlass and exclaimed, "I am going to have a hand in this myself." Unfortunately for the old man's martial enthusiasm, no ram materialized.[21] Insofar as the *Hartford* was concerned, the running of the batteries was proving easy; then, as she reached the sharp bend by the upper battery, the river current swept her off course and toward the batteries. As the vessel began to flop broadside to the current, the Federals deliberately ran her upon the bank.

Once the ship was aground, the engines of the *Albatross* were put in reverse, and the *Hartford* then applied full steam ahead. As the *Albatross* came about she dragged the *Hartford's* stern around, and the bow of the flagship was gradually pointed upstream. The two ships then proceeded to steam upriver as rapidly as possible, not desiring any more contact with the Confederate batteries.[22]

Loyall Farragut, Admiral Farragut's teen-aged son, was on board the *Hartford*. Fleet Surgeon J. M. Foltz said afterwards that just before the action began he went to the admiral and suggested that Loyall be allowed to assist him below in the safest portion of the ship. Foltz explained to Farragut that the boy was not actually in the service and had nothing to gain from exposure on the quarter-deck. Farragut told the doctor in no uncertain terms that the boy was to remain where he was:

No, that will not do. It is true our only child is on board by chance, and he is not in the service; but, being here, he will act as one of my aides, to assist in conveying my orders during the battle, and we will trust in Providence, and *la fortune de la guerre*.[23]

If the *Hartford* had escaped virtually unscathed from Confederate fire, the second ship in line, the *Richmond,* was not so fortunate. From the very beginning of the fateful passage this sloop was destined for ill luck. While following in the rear of the *Hartford,* some seconds before the firing began, the *Richmond's* crew were shocked to hear a cry of terror. Lieutenant Edward Terry immediately yelled, "Man overboard. Throw him a rope." A crewman had fallen from the *Hartford* and was being swept to his death in the current. Despite the efforts of Terry, it was impossible to rescue the man. The *Richmond* proceeded on her way up the stream with the cries of the stricken man ringing in the ears of those aboard. Then there was silence.[24]

The quiet of the night was shattered as the guns began to roar. The *Richmond* blazed away, her double-shotted guns spattering the Confederates with grape and canister. Johnny Rebs on the west bank sprayed the *Richmond* and *Genesee* with musket fire, which the gunners on the double-ender quickly replied to with a port broadside. Battle damage was still fairly light, but "dense clouds of smoke began to envelop the river, shutting out from view the several vessels." The order was given, "Boys, don't fire till you see the flash from the enemy's guns." Visibility was still poor and the officers were having trouble spotting the Rebels. An officer on the topgallant forecastle, spotting a muzzle flash, called out, "Ready with the port gun." The Union sailors brought the heavy gun to bear and prepared to fire, when Lieutenant Terry cried, "Hold on, you are about to fire into the *Hartford.*" Only the muzzle flash from the *Hartford's* guns, which had revealed her spars and rigging to the alert Terry, had prevented a disaster. The great clouds of smoke so completely enveloped the ship that it was necessary to cease firing several times.[25]

Poor visibility or not, Confederate gunners were getting the range, and suddenly a shell entered the forward starboard gunport, killing boatswain's mate John Howard.[26] The *Richmond* had reached the turn in the river and was preparing to steam past to safety when pandemonium broke loose. A shot struck the berth deck, tore through a pile of hawsers and clothes bags, went through the engine room, and ripped the lever of the port safety valve open. Hot steam sprayed the fire room and berth deck, and the pressure dropped to a mere nine pounds.[27] To add to the macabre situation, a cannon shot tore away the left leg of Lieutenant Boyd Cummings, executive officer of the *Richmond*.[28] Almost at the same moment, the *Richmond* staggered as a terrific explosion off the stern splashed water thirty feet in the air. Commander James Alden reported that the explosion was caused by a torpedo, but it was probably a bursting shell.[29]

Her power virtually gone, the *Richmond* began falling back. With the aid of her plucky consort, the *Genesee*, she turned about and began the long trip back past the batteries. Passing close to the east bank, the two ships came under the bluff, where they were protected from cannon fire for a few moments. One Yankee sailor defiantly cried out, "Now let us see you hit us." The Confederates obliged as the two ships pulled back into the channel on their way south, and a shell exploded in the wardroom of the *Genesee*. The double-ender caught fire, but the flames were quickly extinguished. The two ships escaped without further serious harm.[30]

The *Richmond* was hopelessly crippled. She made it to Profit Island, where she remained out of the rest of the fight. The *Genesee*, although damaged, was intact and would soon be back in the thick of the fray.

Third in the order of attack, the *Monongahela* and her consort, the *Kineo*, also ran into trouble. Shortly after the two ships came under fire, a plunging shot from the shore batteries hit the *Kineo*, and she ceased responding to her wheel. With shot and shell flying around, a man was lowered over the stern of the gunboat into the water. He reported that the rudder had been jammed by a solid shot, thus disabling the vessel. The two ships steamed on until they reached the turn, when the *Monongahela* promptly ran aground. Under the impact of the blow, all but one of the hawsers tore loose and the *Kineo* kept going, only to run aground herself about a hundred feet further on. By reversing their engines, the Federals soon backed the little gunboat into deep water. After great difficulty in maneuvering, the *Kineo* succeeded in backing down to her more powerful consort. Using the one hawser that had not been torn apart, she dragged the *Monongahela* into the main current.[31] Aground, the *Monongahela* presented a fat target, which the Confederate gunners proceeded to tear up; if the *Kineo* had not pulled her off, she would have surely been destroyed. Confederate fire disabled two of the 32-pound broadside guns, as well as knocking out one of the 11-inch pivot guns. Then a shot struck the *Monongahela's* bridge, throwing Captain McKinstry to the deck injured.[32]

After towing the *Monongahela* off, Lieutenant John Watters, finding it impossible to steer the *Kineo,* let her drift downstream out of action. Damaged, but still full of fight, the *Monongahela* fought her way upstream until a crank-pin became heated. With her engines thus out of order, she also began to drift.[33] Both ships reached Profit Island by 3:30 A.M., the *Kineo* with disabled engines.[34]

Of the first six ships, only the *Hartford* and the *Albatross* had run the batteries successfully; the other four had taken a pounding. But the fate in store for the last Federal ship was the worst of all. Steaming past the batteries, the old *Mississippi* plodded along, trading shots with the Confederates. Her gunners could only aim at the muzzle flashes of the Confederate guns, because of the great clouds of smoke which covered the river. Near the bend in the river, the crew became alarmed as a dim shadow flitted through the smoke clouds. Believing it to be a Confederate ship, they wanted to give her a broadside; however, Captain Melancton Smith realized the Southerners had no vessel that large on the river, and he refused his men permission to fire. The vessel was the disabled *Richmond,* which was being towed out of action by the *Genesee.*[35]

To heighten the confusion, the *Richmond's* gunners, who did not know their ship had been turned about, fired at the flashes of the *Mississippi's* guns. Excited as they were, the gunners' aim was poor and the *Mississippi* escaped from this incident unscarred. Suddenly the cry of "Torpedoes!" rang out. Fortunately, young George Dewey, the executive officer of the *Mississippi,* and the other officers realized that the "torpedo explosions" were only mortar shells striking the river nearby and splashing the deck of the *Mississippi* with water. Then someone screamed, "They're firing chain-shot at us!" Again it was a case of mistaken identity. The men had merely seen a pair of bombs passing by together, with the two lit fuses giving the odd "effect of being part of the same projectile." [36]

The battle was getting lively and the *Mississippi's* troubles were only starting. The destiny of this venerable veteran was in the hands of the pilot, who faced the task of guiding the vessel past the deadly shoal point. The pilot, believing the shoal had been passed, called out, "Starboard the helm! Full speed ahead!" His calculations were immediately found to be in error; the *Mississippi* ran aground. The vessel was listing badly. Captain Smith tried to back her off, using full power, but the *Mississippi* was stuck. Smith ordered the port battery run in to correct the list. The Confederates zeroed their pieces in and began raking the old lady from bow to stern. The bonfires which had been lighted on the west bank outlined the *Mississippi* clearly, making her an easy mark.

Dewey found Captain Smith on the deck, quite cool, in the act of lighting a cigar. He casually remarked to his young executive officer, "Well, it doesn't look as if we could get her off." Dewey emphatically agreed, "No, it does not." [37]

Confederate gunners, using hot shot, ignited the forward storeroom and the flames soon threatened the magazine. The only course of action left was to abandon ship and save the wounded. Three of the ship's boats were intact, and the sick and badly wounded were sent ashore in these. The scene was one of wild confusion as the flames of the stricken ship lit up the night. A rifle shot, probably from Confederate Battery No. I, tore the howitzer from the *Mississippi's* maintop and flung it clear of the ship into the river. Some of the men escaped by swimming to shore from the badly damaged ship. As the fire reached the larboard guns they were discharged. From the ship's safety valve came a steady shriek of escaping steam to add to the terrible din. Finally, the *Mississippi* floated off from the shoal point and drifted downstream, a funeral pyre for the dead men aboard. Shortly after 5 A.M., March 15, 1863, the ship exploded with a tremendous roar that was heard for miles.[38]

The first battle of Port Hudson had been an extremely noisy affair. All through the fight the six mortar schooners kept up a hot fire on the Confederate batteries, which actually resulted in no casualties. The big 13-inch shells made a tremendous amount of noise, but the gunners were somewhat lacking in accuracy. The *Essex* and *Sachem* were too far away to aim properly and caused no damage. The concentrated fire from the *Mississippi, Hartford, Monongahela, Richmond, Genesee, Albatross,* and *Kineo* caused exactly two Confederate casualties. One lieutenant was slightly wounded in the arm, and a private was wounded in the foot. The Confederate casualty list was a tribute to Union gunnery, which although loud was not very deadly. Not a single Confederate gun was damaged.[39]

If the Confederate artillerymen had a busy night, Southern steamboat men had a night that was more frightening than anything else. At the beginning of the battle two Red River transports were unloading at the Port Hudson wharf. As the shooting commenced, panic and confusion broke out on board these two little ships. Between screaming women and cursing men, the ships' officers managed to get their steamers en route to Thompson's Creek and some degree of safety. As the two transports slipped away from the wharf, General Gardner came running up to Battery No. I, and, observing the lights on the vessels, concluded they were Union gunboats. He immediately called out to Captain J. F. Whitfield, "Why don't you fire on those boats?" Private John Hearn, who failed to recognize the general in the darkness, snarled back, "They are our transports, you infernal thief." Gardner did not reply, apparently concluding that under the circumstances it was best to be a little hard of hearing.[40]

The three-hour battle was over, both sides claiming the victory. During the course of the engagement the *Hartford* had 2 killed and 2 wounded; the *Richmond,* 3 killed and 12 wounded; the *Monongahela,* 6 killed and 21 wounded; the *Mississippi,* out of a total of 297 men, lost 64 killed or missing.[41] Apparently there were no casualties on board the gunboats, although they were struck several times.

The naval action proved that the Port Hudson batteries could not be silenced by naval gunfire and that it would be necessary to use army forces to secure the Port from the landward side, although the possibility of an amphibious assault on the landing under the cover of the guns of the *Essex* was not precluded. The most significant part of the operation was that Farragut had passed the batteries with two warships and would be able to disrupt the communications of the Trans-Mississippi Department.

V

Spring Lull

GENERAL Banks returned to Baton Rouge after Farragut ran the Port Hudson batteries on March 14. For the time Banks forgot Port Hudson. From Baton Rouge he again sent a large detachment of troops into that portion of Louisiana lying west of the Mississippi River known as the Teche country, advancing as far as Alexandria on the Red River. The purpose of his expedition was to achieve three military objectives: to destroy General Richard Taylor's command, to secure a land route to the Red River, and to pick up provisions and horses. The general himself went to New Orleans, leaving behind in Baton Rouge part of his command under General Augur. Although Banks planned to return to Port Hudson at a later date, in the meantime he awaited word from General Grant in regard to the future reduction of the river stronghold with their combined forces, after which he planned to lead his own army to aid Grant in reducing Vicksburg.

Affairs at Port Hudson again took on a quiescent status, and the Confederates lost several opportunities of crossing troops over the river and co-operating with General Taylor. Facing only the reduced garrison at Baton Rouge, Gardner could have detached one or two infantry brigades to aid Taylor. The Confederates could easily have ferried troops across the river at Port Hudson, using the vessels *Starlight* and *Red Chief*. With reinforcements from Gardner, Taylor might well have been able to defeat Banks in the Teche country. And it would have been a simple matter for the troops to return to Port Hudson with only a few days' notice, considering the Federals' lack of forces to patrol the area and the Southerners' familiarity with the countryside. One of the Confederate officers, Lieutenant Howard Wright, later wrote that Gardner's inactivity may have been caused by the Jackson, Mississippi, authorities, who were jealous of subordinate officers and would not let them act independently. Wright also stated that "it was notorious that the most important matters of current business had to be sent on to Jackson for the inspection and approval of an officer too far removed to be able to judge them correctly, thereby causing vexatious delays." [1]

Gardner's most serious problem was that of supply. Forage was scarce on the east side of the river, and little could be brought over from the west side because of the presence of Union cavalry. Several skirmishes between Union and Confederate cavalry occurred during searches for forage, but no important fighting took place. On March 20 the *Monongahela* and the *Genesee* steamed up and shelled Port Hudson, causing no damage. The mortar boats, the *Essex,* and several small gunboats also occasionally sprinkled the Port with high explosives. [2]

On March 24 the Federals set fire to a sugar mill opposite Port Hudson, but retired after the Confederate batteries fired on them. The same day a group of Federal cavalry went up the river and attacked a Confederate vessel, the steamer *Hope,* which was loaded with six hundred barrels of molasses. This force was led by Captain J. M. Magee of the unattached Massachusetts Cavalry. After destroying the vessel, Magee and part of his men proceeded to Hermitage Landing, where they found over a thousand barrels of molasses, which they also destroyed. He and his men burned a Confederate machine shop which was being used to repair Rebel guns and a government granary containing fifteen thousand bushels of corn intended for Port Hudson. They also destroyed a drugstore, which was supplied with many valuable drugs, a post office, and several other buildings. [3]

With no apparent threat of attack on Port Hudson, and a great need for troops in the Vicksburg campaign, General John C. Pemberton, Confederate commander at Vicksburg, on May 4 ordered Gardner to send 5,000 infantry to that place. Gardner answered on May 5 that he would comply with Pemberton's request, and the next day additional units under his command were ordered to leave Port Hudson for Jackson and Vicksburg.[4]

At the end of March the Port Hudson garrison consisted roughly of 16,000 men, organized into five brigades under Generals W. N. R. Beall, Abraham Buford, John Gregg, S. B. Maxey, and Albert Rust. The river fortifications mounted nineteen or twenty guns (10-inch Columbiads to 24-pounder siege guns) manned by three artillery battalions, with thirteen light batteries, numbering over seventy pieces.[5] On April 29, 1863, General Gardner sent Pemberton the following report: "Effective infantry 8,600, artillery 1,700, cavalry 1,400, including Ponchatoula." [6] The difference in number in the two reports was due to the detachment of several bodies of troops north to Mississippi.

In the meantime, General Grant launched a cavalry raid, under the command of Colonel Benjamin H. Grierson, to divert Pemberton's attention from the Mississippi while Grant marched down the west side to cross the river south of Vicksburg. The day after Commodore David Porter's boats ran the Vicksburg batteries, Grierson's expedition left La Grange, Tennessee. Sixteen days later the Union cavalry crossed Williams' Bridge and reached Baton Rouge, after one of the longest and most effective cavalry raids of the war. On an order from Pemberton, General Gardner sent his cavalry and infantry to intercept Grierson, but high water and a communications mix-up prevented the main bodies from catching him. Major James DeBaun, with part of the Ninth Louisiana Partisan Ranger Battalion, did shoot up Grierson's party at Wall's Bridge near Osyka, Mississippi, but the outnumbered rangers were forced to retreat.[7]

On May 8, 1863, Farragut left the *Hartford* under Porter's command and journeyed south to take command of Union naval forces lying below Port Hudson, enabling him to support Banks's campaign against that place. The Union fleet commenced operations before the land forces, taking positions that day on the river about four and a half miles below the Port. The mortar boats opened fire around two o'clock in the afternoon, trying to get the range of the Confederate river batteries, numbered from

I to XI, north to south. Most of the shells fell on Battery No. X, a 32-pounder battery, and Lieutenant J. W. Kearney's Parrott battery, No. XI. Several long-range mortar shells fell on Lieutenant O. Rodriguez's battery, No. IX, and Captain W. N. Coffin's two rifled 24-pounders, No. VIII. But as the distance was too far for accurate aim, the firing did no harm.[8]

Upon hitting the ground, many of the shells buried themselves in the earth; others veered, landing great distances away. Still others exploded, "uprooting the earth like a small volcano, and throwing out pieces of roots and other substances which had probably never seen the light of day before." [9] The defenders had no place to go for protection; everyone stayed at his post, doing what had to be done, while fragments of shells flew in all directions. Many projectiles struck the trees laterally instead of with their percussion caps foremost, and failed to detonate.

As soon as the mortar boats took up their positions, Colonel De Gournay received permission to take four cannon down to Troth's Landing to make an attack on the Union vessels. De Gournay's force consisted of a 24-pound rifle manned by troops from his battalion, a 4.62-inch brass rifle (called "The Baby") manned by members of Company K, First Alabama Regiment, commanded by Lieutenant C. E. Tuttle,[10] and 12-pound and 20-pound Parrott rifles manned by troops from Miles' Legion.

As darkness fell on May 9, the Confederates began the construction of a gun position near Troth's Landing, and by dawn a redoubt eighteen inches deep and twelve by twenty-four feet in size had been finished. The dirt taken from the redoubt was heaped up in front, making a parapet which the two larger guns could just peek over. The two smaller cannon were placed in an old gun position a few hundred yards lower down. It was not until 4 A.M. that all the works were completed and the guns made ready for action. The tired but expectant gunners were standing around when the Union warships opposite them suddenly let go with a tremendous blast. Confederates scattered in all directions. But it turned out to be a false alarm; the Federals were only firing on the Port Hudson river batteries.

Dawn broke, and the iron and brass monsters were brought to bear on the U.S.S. *Essex.* Colonel De Gournay shouted, "Fire!" The percussion shell from "The Baby" exploded just short of the *Essex,* spattering the ironclad with fragments. The Confederates also blazed away at the mortar boats, but the latter were moored close under the bluff and were immune from the worst of the shelling. Within minutes the Union mortar schooners returned the Confederate fire. Their great 13-inch shells made short arcs through the air, sprinkling the Southerners with fragments as the iron balls detonated. Some of the big shells sank into the soft earth before exploding, spraying the Louisianians and Alabamans with dirt. The *Essex* chimed in with her guns, and minutes later the *Richmond* burst a big shell near the beleaguered gunners.[11]

After a heavy exchange of fire, the *Richmond* abandoned her anchorage and steamed straight for the Confederates. The crew of "The Baby" put a shot through her rigging, and the crew of the 24-pounder slammed their last round into the sloop's hull. The Parrotts were out of ammunition and "The Baby" broke down; the Confederates could only wait as the powerful sloop steamed toward them, her guns blazing. When within about four hundred yards, the *Richmond* came about, discharged both broadsides, and steamed back to her anchorage. The *Essex* and the mortar schooners ceased firing. The Federals apparently decided they were only wasting ammunition. The Confederates, their ammunition exhausted, hitched their guns up and withdrew northward to Port Hudson without further incident. Despite the ferocity of the fire, losses on both sides were trifling, amounting only to a few wounded and minor damage to several of the Union ships.[12]

On this same night a soldier, standing on the parapet of Battery No. IX, received a direct hit from "one of these descending thunder-bolts," driving his body through the wooden battery floor into the ground below and leaving only his feet sticking out.[13] This was the Confederates' first casualty from a shell. The next casualties were on May 17, when a shell entered near the crest of one of the lower parapets, burying itself in the ground beneath a spot where four of De Gournay's men were sitting. The explosion that followed threw the men into the air, killing three of them and wounding the other. Another mortar shell hit soon after the burial of these men, bursting in the graveyard among the coffins and throwing bodies around. Two more Rebs lost legs from being struck by fragments of exploding shells. The network of ditches and ravines was ravaged by shot and shell; caverns twelve to fifteen feet deep, wider and bigger than ordinary cellars, were opened.[14]

During this period, while Banks was maneuvering in western Louisiana and the mortar schooners were dropping frequent shells on the Port Hudson works, life in the garrison had its lighter moments. The men of Captain C. E. Fenner's battery at Troth's Landing took time off on occasion to break the monotony of camp life. In the early hours of a morning, well past midnight, these men played marbles on a flat memorial slab in a nearby cemetery. The gunners wound up the night by "leap-frogging," "seven-upping," and holding a foot race to see which one would get to sleep on the big flat tomb, which was dry and more comfortable than the damp Louisiana earth.[15]

An interesting incident occurred during an afternoon bombardment by the fleet in middle May. A shell exploded in the river with such force that it caused scores of fish to rise to the surface, where they lay floating on top of the water, stunned. Some of the Confederate soldiers made a quick trip out to the spot in skiffs, gathered up fish, and returned to the shore with their valuable catch. The Federals had aided the enterprising Confederates in their ceaseless search for something to eat.[16]

The bombardment continued nearly every night, and sometimes the Federals shelled the Port during the day. The Confederates soon learned how to determine where the shells were going to strike and how to get out of the way. This type of action by the Union fleet kept up until May 24, when the mortar boats adopted a system of throwing shells at regular intervals. The bombardment caused little damage, however—mainly because the Port Hudson defenses encompassed such a large area.

Pemberton's call for reinforcements in early May had weakened the garrison. The brigades of Rust and Buford left on May 4, and John Gregg's brigade followed the next day. General Maxey departed on May 8, and Miles' Legion followed just behind. Shortly after Colonel William R. Miles and his men went out, Gardner and his staff followed, leaving only General Beall's brigade and the heavy artillery at Port Hudson.[17]

When Banks realized that most of the garrison had withdrawn, he decided the time was ripe for an attack. A rapid advance was begun. The Federals hoped to take the Port by surprise, enabling them to gain both the works and heavy guns in good condition.

General Gardner had not gone many miles toward his Mississippi destination when he received the following dispatch from Pemberton: "Return to Port Hudson with two thousand troops and hold it to the last. President says both places must be held."[18] Obeying orders, Gardner returned. Colonel Miles was also ordered to return at once. Preparations were begun in view of the possibility of a siege. Provisions were obtained, though not in large quantities. Three hundred head of beef, four hundred head of sheep, and four hundred bushels of corn were brought in from across the river by the night of May 21, despite the presence of the Federal fleet.[19]

During March, April, and May considerable correspondence took place between Banks and Grant in regard to the co-ordination of their forces. But it was not until May 12, when Banks was at Alexandria, that for the first time he was in direct and comparatively rapid communication with Grant. This letter, written by Grant on May 10, who was now in the thick of his Vicksburg campaign, explained to Banks the impossibility of sending any troops. Grant emphasized the fact that he could not spare a man and asked Banks to aid him.[20]

Banks deliberated as to what course of action he should take —whether to go after the Confederates in his front, to turn toward Vicksburg as requested by Grant, or to Port Hudson. To move on Vicksburg would take too much time and would leave New Orleans open to attack from Port Hudson. The only feasible plan was to strike Port Hudson.

On May 19 the Union Chief of Staff, Henry W. Halleck, wrote

to Banks urging him to abandon his campaign in Louisiana and to unite with Grant in order to prevent his being crushed by Joseph E. Johnston's and Pemberton's armies.[21] Four days later Halleck sent another letter to Banks telling him of his disappointment that the two armies had not united and expressing fear that the Southerners would destroy either Banks or Grant if they did not quickly unite.[22] Such was the existing communications problem that by the time Halleck's letters were written, Banks and Grant were committed to their own plans for the final operations on the Mississippi River—Grant at Vicksburg and Banks before Port Hudson. There was no backing out.

General Johnston, departmental commander of the Confederate military area, wrote to Gardner on May 19, 1863:

Lieutenant-General Pemberton has been compelled to fall back to Vicksburg and abandon Haynes' Bluff, so that your position is no longer valuable. It is important also that all the troops in the department should be concentrated as soon as possible. Evacuate Port Hudson forthwith and move with your troops toward Jackson, to join other troops which I am uniting. Bring all the field pieces that you have, with means of transportation, heavy guns and their ammunition had better be destroyed, as well as the other property you may be unable to remove.[23]

It is possible that Banks moved on Port Hudson too soon. George S. Denison, in a letter to Salmon P. Chase, wrote later that Banks's private secretary told him Port Hudson would have been evacuated had Banks been just a few hours later in getting there; that Gardner had the order to evacuate in his pocket, and had begun executing it when the Federals appeared.[24] This is partially corroborated by a Southern source. Colonel John Logan wrote to General Johnston on May 29, 1863, telling the departmental commander that Gardner had not evacuated Port Hudson because the place was "invested" before the order was received.[25]

While Banks's army was moving closer to Port Hudson, the Confederate cavalry had not been idle. Colonel Frank Powers, chief of cavalry, had under him Thomas R. Stockdale's Mississippi Battalion, John B. Cage's Louisiana Battalion, the Eleventh and Seventeenth Arkansas Mounted Infantry (combined), commanded by Colonel John G. Griffith, and W. H. Garland's Battalion. This force was assisted by Major James Aiken's Ninth Tennessee Battalion, 350 men. The cavalrymen were armed with shotguns, Belgian rifles, and the like, with the exception of the mounted infantry, who all had rifles.[26]

Since Baton Rouge was too far from the place of action to keep Federal supplies, Springfield Landing became the Union supply base. Steamships and other vessels brought in supplies and ammunition from Baton Rouge and New Orleans. The *Kineo,* stationed near Profit Shute, patrolled the river, and a detachment of troops from the Third Louisiana Native Guard, with artillery, guarded the road to the landing. General T. W. Sherman was stationed nearby on the road, which had been repaired by the colored troops. A communications system between the land and naval forces ran from Blair's Church to the *Monongahela,* which lay just off the head of Profit Island. A signal corps detachment was stationed close by in a cottonwood grove a few yards from the landing.[27]

On May 20 General Augur moved the remainder of his troops up to join N. A. M. Dudley so as to cover Sherman's landing at Springfield and to meet the advance of the main body of the Nineteenth Army Corps from Bayou Sara. Included in Augur's forces now were Dudley, Edward Chapin, Benjamin H. Grierson, J. F. Godfrey's squadron, composed of troops C and E of the Louisiana Cavalry, two sections of Jacob B. Rawles's battery, R. E. Holcomb's battery, and one section of Albert G. Mack's, commanded by Sergeant D. W. McConnell. Augur himself was on the Bayou Sara Road awaiting the arrival of Banks. The forces under Colonel Dudley proceeded toward the crossing of the Plains Store and Bayou Sara roads for the purpose of seizing the Confederate's "line of retreat" and to clear the way for General Banks.[28]

VI

The Investment

ON May 20 the approach of Augur's forces was announced by brisk skirmishes with Confederate cavalry pickets. That night Banks began crossing the river at Bayou Sara with his veterans of the Teche campaign. Early the next morning Colonel Powers' cavalry, with a few companies of infantry, and George Abbay's Mississippi Battery skirmished with the Federals in the vicinity of the Plains Store at the edge of the woods that formed the southern boundary of the Plains.

About noon Gardner sent an order to Colonel Miles directing him to take four hundred men and reconnoiter the Federals, relieving Powers to link up with Colonel Logan. Miles's infantry, supported by Boone's Louisiana Battery, marched out to meet Augur's advancing unit. Miles placed two companies under Major James T. Coleman, and Colonel F. B. Brand was assigned the three other companies.[1]

In the heavy thicket that "masked the crossroads and formed the western border of the plain," Miles's force met Augur's. Colonel Dudley was on the right side of the road leading from the Plains Store to Port Hudson, supporting Holcomb's guns; Colonel Chapin was on the left, supporting Rawles's. The Forty-eighth Massachusetts, posted in columns on both sides of the road, gave way in confusion as Miles's unit charged through the thicket. Momentarily, the Forty-eighth fell back through the advancing Forty-ninth Massachusetts, hindering the action of that regiment, but the One Hundred Sixteenth New York made a brisk charge, restoring order.[2] The engagement degenerated into a simple fire fight until Coleman stormed a section of Yankee artillery, bringing on a desperate battle for the possession of the two guns. With the guns' horses dead, the Confederates were unable to drag the cannon off and were forced to retreat after a fierce Yankee counterattack. Heavily outnumbered, Miles fought for over an hour before giving the order to fall back. The Yanks made no pursuit, and the Southerners were able to carry off all their wounded. Miles's losses were 12 killed and 36 wounded. Augur lost 15 dead, 14 captured, and 71 wounded.[3] The action was called the "Battle of the Plains Store."

The two-story building—the first floor serving as a country store and the second as a Masonic hall—took a severe drubbing during the battle. A cannon shot hit a piano, "playing Hail Columbia with variations," while "solid trees were cut down" and the ground was covered with "bushels of grape and canister."[4]

On Friday, May 22, Colonel J. H. Wingfield's cavalry skirmished with Banks's advance, but the Southerners were forced back to Sandy Creek. Gardner had not anticipated an attack from this area north of the town, with its heavy timber and swampy soil, and had erected no fortifications there. The Federals were only able to advance by cutting roads through the rugged terrain.

The fighting was getting closer to the Confederate fortifications. While some of the troops at their batteries listened to the sounds of battle in the distance, Gardner rode up, unattended, as usual, and asked, "Are you all ready here?" The men answered that they were ready and waiting. The general pointed toward the crack of the enemy's fire and said, "The enemy are coming, but mark you, many a one will get to H—l before he does to Port Hudson."[5]

On Friday, May 22, Colonel I. G. W. Steedman of the First Alabama Volunteers was placed in command of the entire left wing of the works at Port Hudson. The right wing was assigned to Colonel Miles; the center was given to General Beall. Steedman took up a position half a mile in advance of the Confederates' main works on the road leading past the commissary depot and grist mill. A battalion of cavalry, Wingfield's, and a section of the Watson Battery were ordered to report to Steedman.

Colonel Ben Johnson was placed in command of the advanced works on the right. Steedman's command extended to the Mississippi River on the extreme left.[6] Johnson was to prevent the enemy from advancing as long as possible.

Steedman had been ordered by Gardner to "observe the enemy and to oppose his advance upon our works, but without risking a serious engagement." [7] Through the efforts of Wingfield's cavalry, Steedman learned that the Federals were advancing on all approaches to the Confederate defenses. Wingfield ordered a picket of ten men to the gate at the Chambers plantation on the Bayou Sara Road. The Federals drove Wingfield's men back and advanced toward Aberger's plantation. Wingfield spread out his troops, trying to hold back the advancing Yanks.[8]

Immediately Steedman threw out a line of skirmishers, consisting of four companies of the First Alabama under Colonel M. B. Locke, and for two days there was skirmishing with the Federal advance guard along Steedman's entire front. Steedman received reinforcements of three battalions—a battalion from the First Mississippi and one from the Fifteenth Arkansas, commanded respectively by Major Thomas Johnston and Lieutenant Colonel Lee; also the battalion of the provost guard, commanded by Captain J. R. Wilson.[9]

Banks completed the investment of Port Hudson on May 23. But even as his soldiers drew their lines tightly together, Steedman counterattacked. His forces encountered the Federals in several skirmishes as they descended the bluff into the "swamp canopied high above with the luxuriant foliage of a giant forest." [10] The Federal pickets, perceiving the advance of the Confederates, ceased firing and hid behind trees. The Confederate squads pushed onward through briars, brush, logs, and other obstacles. When they were within a few yards of a slough of heavy underbrush which formed the "farther margin of this clearing," [11] the crack of Union fire and musketry rang out. Being exposed to a hidden enemy, the Southerners had to return the fire without a chance of aiming. Locke ordered his troops to fall back, thinking the odds were too risky. After gathering up their dead and wounded, they fell back with no apparent gain.

Steedman felt it was not prudent to attempt any further advance that night. Placing pickets upon his advanced line, he withdrew his command to its original position.

A freak accident occurred on the night of Sunday, May 24. A Minié ball cut out the letter C on Steedman's sword belt, leaving only the S. Steedman was not wearing the sword at the time, Colonel Locke having picked it up by mistake, and it was he who had the narrow escape.[12]

Meanwhile, the *Hartford, Albatross, Sachem,* and *Arizona* lay at anchor just beyond the bend near Port Hudson, and down below, anchored just off Profit Island, lay the *Monongahela, Richmond, Genesee, Essex,* and the mortar flotilla. These vessels kept watch by means of picket boats, looking for and hoping to intercept any communication coming into the Confederate garrison.[13] Their frequent bombardments were exceedingly noisy. During a two and a half hour shelling on May 24, De Gournay's command fired twenty-four shots at the mortar boats and gunboats, but the range was so great that little damage was done. One shell from Captain W. B. Seawall's battery struck the *Monongahela* on her bow. The Confederate batteries were hit with fragments of mortar and rifle shells, and the gun carriage at Battery No. X was slightly damaged, though not enough to disable it.[14]

Colonel Miles's line was comparatively quiet that Sunday; however, three of his men were wounded and three were killed by the Federal bombardment. The lull was temporary, and on Monday, over to the left of Troth's, there was plenty of action. A demonstration was made by Federal cavalry and infantry, then by cavalry alone. Both attacks were dispersed by Confederate artillery. After being driven off the field, the Federals came forward under a flag of truce. Miles sent Captain R. M. Hewitt and Lieutenant B. W. Clark to meet the white flag, but before they reached it, the flag was taken away and the Federals returned to the woods carrying litters bearing dead and wounded soldiers. Although the use of the white flag was illicit, Miles did not fire on it. Gardner notified Banks of the violation, requesting that orders "be given to prevent the like occurring again," and said he would "be compelled to fire upon the flag used for such purposes." [15]

As of the morning of May 25 Banks's order of battle was, from left to right, T. W. Sherman (whose left flank rested on the east bank of the Mississippi River), Christopher Augur (holding a line running across the Plains Store road), Cuvier Grover (entrenched along the Jackson road), Halbert Paine, Godfrey Weitzel, and William Dwight (respectively holding positions in front of the Confederate rifle pits on the left).[16] On the afternoon of May 25 General Paine ordered Colonel Edward Prince to Thompson's Creek to destroy some Confederate vessels. Prince, with two hundred men of his own regiment, two companies of infantry of the Thirty-first Massachusetts, and the left section of the First Maine battery, arrived at the creek. Using the artillery and infantry as a reserve, he dismounted his cavalry, then proceeded up the stream. The position of the vessels was practically inaccessible because of the bayous on either side of the creek; however, the *Starlight* and *Red Chief* were captured. The steamers had been of great service to the Southerners and both were in perfect running condition. About twenty-five Confederate prisoners were captured along with the vessels.[17]

On May 25 the Federals placed about ninety pieces of artillery in position; however, the Confederates were not napping. Steedman's skirmishers were constantly busy as the advance troops of Banks's army hit along his entire front. Steedman advanced his lines about five hundred yards to a good position and formed in line of battle. With the section of the Watson Battery, commanded by Lieutenant E. A. Toledano, covering the road, the infantry were posted both to the right and left under cover of the crest of a hill, throwing up temporary works. Standing before this line of battle was an open space of about ten acres, which was studded with heavy timber. To hold this point Steedman had about six hundred men.[18]

Steedman was convinced that his line in the vicinity of the commissary depot, arsenal, and grist mill would receive the enemy's big attack. After he and Gardner discussed this possibility and the need of fortifications there, the commanding general ordered all the available tools and Negroes placed at the disposal of Lieutenant Fred Y. Dabney, chief engineer, who at once laid out a plan of defense. By dawn Tuesday, considerable progress had been made. A battery of four pieces was mounted on the hill in the immediate vicinity of the commissary depot. The emergency being great, this work was pushed with energy all day Tuesday, and by the dawn of Wednesday an imperfect line of rifle pits had been thrown up to protect the most exposed positions on the left wing. Where rifle pits were wanting, breastworks of logs were quickly constructed.[19]

On May 26 a shell from a Parrott on the *Monongahela* dismounted one of the Confederates' 10-inch Columbiads, putting it out of action for several days. On this same day the Confederates commenced shelling the willow swamp where the Federal engineers were completing their last bridge.[20]

Contrary to expectations, the Federals did not push their advance on May 26, giving the Southerners an extra day to dig in. Probably if Banks had attacked the garrison in full force on that day, he would have won a victory. There was very little firing as both sides were busy preparing for the work of the next day. Being on the defensive, Steedman's men slept on their arms that night.

To prepare for the expected Union assault, Gardner ordered the 24-pound rifles in the river batteries moved to the Confederate earthworks covering the landward side, the last gun being moved on the night of May 26. He then reapportioned the garrison out among his three capable senior officers—Steedman, Beall, and Miles. Steedman had the Tenth, Fifteenth, and Eighteenth Arkansas, the Thirty-ninth Mississippi, the First Alabama Infantry, one company of Wingfield's cavalry, A. J. Herod's battery, and one section each of Bradford's battery and the Watson battery. To defend the center Beall had the First Mississippi Infantry, the Twelfth and Sixteenth Arkansas, the Forty-ninth Alabama, the First Arkansas Battalion, Abbay's battery, a section of Bradford's battery, and the remainder of the Watson battery. Miles, commanding the right, had the Louisiana Legion, the Special Tennessee Battalion, the Ninth Louisiana

Infantry Battalion, plus the remainder of the Confederate field artillery and all the unattached infantry companies.[21]

With his troops outnumbering those of the Confederate forces, Banks desired a general assault, and he and the division commanders met at his headquarters on the Bayou Sara Road on the night of May 26. No minutes were kept of this meeting, "and to this day its conclusions are a matter of dispute." [22] But Banks seems to have urged immediate action and he emerged from the meeting in high spirits. He issued a set of eleven orders calling for a massive army-navy bombardment of Port Hudson at dawn, or six o'clock, on the following morning. It was apparently his intention for his divisional commanders to launch simultaneous massed infantry attacks during the shelling, but the wording of the attack orders stated only that Augur and Sherman were to "if possible force the enemy's works at the earliest moment." Weitzel was ordered to attack the Confederate left once Augur and Sherman had begun their assaults. Grover was directed to support either Weitzel or Augur, or if he wished, to make an attack of his own. No mention was made of Paine or Dwight in drawing up the order. The confused tone of the order demonstrated Banks's lack of a formal military education. In effect, each of his divisional commanders was free to either attack or to merely hold his present position, according to what he desired.[23]

Apparently Banks left the council with a clear picture of what was to take place on the following morning. If so, he was the only officer there who had that understanding. His divisional commanders had only the foggiest notions as to what their role in the forthcoming battle was to be. The confusion caused by the council was to have disastrous results. The stage was set, however, for a general assault. The one thought in the Unionists' minds was "Port Hudson must be taken tomorrow." [24]

VII

May 27

SHORTLY after dawn on the morning of Wednesday, May 27, 1863, Union army and navy artillery began a heavy bombardment of Port Hudson. Chunks of iron hit the Confederate encampments, mowing down anyone foolish enough to expose himself. Fire rained from the Union left and center, but the Union right, under Generals Weitzel, Grover, Dwight, and Paine, was strangely quiet. The reason for the silence was soon evident. From this quarter the blue-coated columns of Weitzel's division advanced to the attack. Colonel Jacob Van Zandt's brigade (the First Louisiana and the Ninety-first and One Hundred Thirty-first New York) spearheaded the advance, with Weitzel's old brigade, now commanded by Colonel Stephen Thomas, following close behind and slightly to the left.[1]

The Confederate skirmish lines, numbering about five hundred men, under Colonel Locke, engaged Weitzel's troops on the far side of Sandy Creek. The struggle was desperate, and the Confederates were forced to retire across the creek in the face of overwhelming numbers.[2] The Confederates retreated only after being forced out of each position. Every ravine, hollow, gully, and hillside was contested by the retiring Southerners. Often unable to see their enemy, Weitzel's stubborn Yankees continued their advance until they secured a ridge about two hundred yards from the Confederate works. As they occupied the ridge in front of Commissary Hill, from which Locke had withdrawn, Colonel Steedman ordered the four-gun battery on the hill to open fire on the Federals.[3]

Commissary Hill was a key point in the Confederate defense system, as the commissary stores, arsenal, and grist mill were

50

located back of it. Steedman's gunners raked the Federals, but Union sharpshooters picked off many of them and compelled others to seek shelter. A party of Federal riflemen enfiladed the ditch near the abandoned battery and began aiming for the Confederate gunners lying crouched behind the works. Captain S. D. Steedman, brother of Colonel Steedman, was sent to drive the Federals out; he was shot down by a rifle slug which struck him over the heart.[4]

With banners waving and bayonets gleaming in the morning sun, the Union infantry sallied forth from their newly won positions in the woods and on the ridges. Wave after wave of blue-coated soldiers advanced against the Confederate line without a shot being fired. Their ranks thinned, the Confederates fell back to within their earthworks to await the coming assault.

The First Maine Battery and a battery of the First United States Field Artillery, supported by Colonel John Kimball's Fifty-third Massachusetts Infantry, were brought forward to provide covering fire for the advancing Federal soldiers.[5] The Federals came to within forty yards of the Confederate lines before the order to fire rang out. In the words of one Confederate, John A. Kennedy, "We are laying in our rifle-pits, awaiting the hated foe. . . . They will catch it, sure as two and two makes four." [6]

From hundreds of old flintlock muskets they caught it, as blasts of buck and ball swept them back. The Yankees rallied and charged again. The Alabamans and Arkansans drove them back with furious slaughter. Colonel Locke was wounded, but his men never faltered, and the Union advance was stopped.

Because of the difficulties of the terrain and the murderous Confederate fire, Van Zandt's regiments began to drift toward the right, and, to protect his front, General Paine began moving his division into the gap left by Van Zandt.[7] Paine's Third Brigade, under Colonel Oliver P. Gooding, launched an attack on the Tenth Arkansas. Gooding had the Thirty-first and Thirty-eighth Massachusetts and the One Hundred Fifty-sixth New York, but the outnumbered Arkansans broke his assault with deadly volleys of musket fire. The Second Brigade, consisting of the Eighth New Hampshire, the Fourth Wisconsin, the One Hundred Thirty-third and One Hundred Seventy-third New York, all under Colonel Hawkes Fearing, Jr., moved up after Gooding's repulse to finish the job. Although they suffered heavy losses, some of Fearing's men reached the ditch outside the Confederate works and planted their battleflags in the dirt. The New York, New Hampshire, and Wisconsin troops fought desperately, picking off many of the Arkansans, but were eventually driven out of the ditch to more sheltered positions.[8] Colonel E. L. Vaughan's Tenth Arkansas Infantry had taken the worst the Yanks could throw at them, and they had held.

General Paine's attack failed, as had the earlier attack of Weitzel, but the Union forces were still strong enough to continue fighting. To support Weitzel and Paine, General Grover sent the One Hundred Fifty-ninth New York in against the left flank of the position held by Ben Johnson's Fifteenth Arkansas. Heavily outnumbered, the Arkansans permitted the Federals to advance to within thirty yards of their position before opening fire. The Yanks were badly cut up and forced to retreat to cover in the numerous gullies and ravines in front of the Confederate lines, where they began sniping at Johnson's men. Undismayed by the repulse, Grover ordered the Twelfth Maine and the Thirteenth, and Twenty-fifth Connecticut to deliver a two-pronged attack against a portion of Johnson's regiment, located in a series of works on a hill jutting out from the right of the main line. The Yanks struck the face and left side of the works simultaneously.[9] Troops of the Twelfth Maine actually planted their flag on the outside of the parapet of the position, but the Arkansans drove them back after a brief bayonet fight. The three Northern regiments were forced back, and the survivors took shelter in the gullies surrounding the hill and raked the Arkansans with rifle fire. A wild battle raged for several hours, and from the fury of the fighting the hill earned a name—"Fort Desperate." When the battle finally ended, the Yankee dead in front of Fort Desperate numbered between eighty and ninety.[10]

While Grover's main force was battering at Fort Desperate, a smaller group was sent to isolate the Fifteenth Arkansas from the First Alabama by driving a wedge through that portion of the battlefield known as the "Bull Pen," which was virtually undefended.[11]

The Twenty-third Arkansas Infantry, commanded by Colonel O. P. Lyles, had been holding the extreme left of the Confederate center. In the emergency the regiment was swung around behind the Fifteenth Arkansas to take up new positions along the Bull Pen. The Union advance was thus stopped, but at the expense of weakening the Confederate center, where, fortunately, no action was yet underway.[12]

The only other action of note occurring on the Confederate left was the famous attack of Dwight's colored troops.[13] After the failure of the first Union assaults against the Confederate left, Dwight sought to create a diversion in favor of Grover and Paine, and in order to feel out the strength of Colonel W. B. Shelby's force on the extreme left, he ordered Colonel John A. Nelson to commit the First and Third Louisiana Native Guards. Shelby's line "occupied the nearly level crest of a steep bluff that completely dominates the low ground by the sugar-house, where the telegraph road crosses Foster's Creek." [14] Directly in front of the crest, and slightly below it, lay a rugged bluff which jutted sharply to the right. This formed a natural outwork which was practically inaccessible. The ridge was about four hundred yards in length and ran to within two hundred yards of the bridge over Sandy Creek. It was held by Company B, Thirty-ninth Mississippi Infantry (45 men), and a detachment from Wingfield's Ninth Louisiana Cavalry Battalion (15 men), all under the command of Lieutenant S. D. Rhodes.[15]

The main Confederate position was held by six companies of the Thirty-ninth Mississippi Infantry and several field guns.[16] The bridge over Sandy Creek had been burned by the retreating Confederates, but before dawn May 27 black pioneers, probably assisted by Company K, Forty-second Massachusetts Infantry (an engineer company equipped with inflatable rubber pontoons), erected another bridge over the creek. The First and Third Louisiana Native Guards, supported by white troops of Dwight's brigade,[17] crossed the newly completed bridge and began forming for an assault. Union artillerymen of the Sixth Massachusetts Battery brought two brass guns across the bridge to support the Negro troops' advance.[18]

As the Massachusetts men unlimbered their guns, Confederate gunners opened fire with solid shot and forced them to retire across the creek. One of the Union 6-pounders was dismounted and the other was run out of range, taking no further part in the engagement. Colonel Shelby requested fire support from the river batteries, and Captains William B. Seawall and J. F. Whitfield opened up with a 30-pound Parrott and several Columbiads.[19] The colored troops, the First Louisiana leading, continued a steady advance on Shelby's position, though brought under a sharp flanking fire from Lieutenant Rhodes's command. This advance continued until the First Louisiana was within two hundred yards of the Mississippians, when the field guns opened with canister and the excited Mississippi Infantry joined in the fire with their muskets. The First Louisiana fell back in disorder upon the Third, and both regiments retreated in confusion to the north bank of Sandy Creek, near the sugar house.[20]

Exaggerated accounts of the prowess of the colored troops were circulated throughout the North for propaganda purposes. The Negroes were said to have engaged the Mississippians in mortal hand-to-hand combat, fighting with bayonets. "One negro was observed with a rebel soldier in his grasp, tearing the flesh from his face with his teeth, other weapons having failed him. After firing one volley they did not deign to load again, but went in with bayonets, and whenever they had a chance it was all up with the rebels." [21] An illustration in *Harper's Weekly* showed colored troops storming a position bristling with heavy cannon and scores of Confederates armed with bayonets and rifles. One Guard of heroic physical proportions was depicted hoisting the "Stars and Stripes" over the position, while a scrubby looking "Johnny Reb" poised to stab him in the back with a bayonet.[22] According to another observer, the colored troops engaged the Confederate soldiers in desperate hand-to-hand fighting, but were finally overpowered, whereupon about two hundred of them jumped over the edge of the parapet and thus escaped death or capture.[23]

Confederate accounts of the action are radically different from those of Union sources. In general, the evidence is that the colored troops did not fight with any great degree of enthusiasm or skill. A Federal officer, Colonel Halbert S. Greenleaf, Fifty-third Massachusetts, who was present at Port Hudson at the time, stated that the officers had no confidence in the black soldiers and that they, in turn, had no confidence in themselves; the result was an exhibition of cowardice on the part of the entire group.[24]

Many of the white soldiers behaved as poorly as the colored troops, and for a first try, the latter did not do too badly. If the colored troops had fought as hard as some Abolitionists claimed, they would have been annihilated, for the Thirty-ninth Mississippi was an experienced fighting unit, even though poorly equipped. One indication that the Negroes did little in the way of serious fighting is that the Thirty-ninth Mississippi did not suffer a single casualty in the May 27 battle. The effective strength of the Mississippians involved was less than three hundred infantry, and probably two dozen artillerymen.[25] One unfortunate aspect of the attack was that Shelby's men were charged with massacring helpless Negro prisoners.[26] Reports were circulated among the Union forces that the Confederates hanged a number of colored prisoners and tortured others.[27] The Mississippians were accused of nailing them, while they were still alive, to the trees around the bluffs.[28] Lieutenant Daniel P. Smith suggested that most of the colored casualties were caused by Union soldiers shooting the fleeing Negroes down.[29] Lieutenant Howard Wright said, "They broke at our fire and clustered behind the willow trees apparently too panic-stricken either to advance or run . . . On account of white troops behind them they probably had some difficulty in getting away, but in fifteen minutes after they first appeared none of them were to be seen except the dead and those who were too badly wounded to crawl off . . ."[30] The charges of Southern atrocities were refuted by several Northern officers, as well as by the surgeon who treated General Sherman.[31]

No Confederate accounts speak of any Negro troops approaching closer than two hundred yards of the Confederate works, and none mentions any prisoners being taken, although possibly a few wounded were picked up after the battle. Apparently the atrocity stories were invented by anti-slavery leaders to inflame public opinion and to stimulate sympathy for the enlistment of non-white troops into the United States Army.

In memory of the attack, the first great action in which colored troops participated in the war, Northern poets felt called upon to indulge their feelings in lyrical rhymes about the incident. The following imitation of Lord Tennyson's *Charge of the Light Brigade* is probably the worst:

> "Niggers won't fight," ah, ha!
> "Niggers won't fight," ah, ha!
> "They are no good for war,
> One in a hundred."
> Let Mississippi's shore,
> Flooded with negro gore,
> Echo back evermore—
> "See our six hundred!" [32]

By 11 A.M. the fighting on the Union right (Confederate left) was over. The troops of Dwight, Paine, Grover, and Weitzel had secured a few minor positions, but no decisive advantage had been gained. More than a dozen fine Northern regiments had been chewed up in the fighting. Still, the Federals possessed many troops capable of engaging Colonel Steedman's command, if there were any possible hope of victory. The Union left and center had failed to move forward, and General Weitzel, commanding the right wing, decided to wait for Sherman and Augur to attack before trying anything further with his somewhat battered soldiers.

All during the morning, as Weitzel and his fellow officers tried to smash the Confederate left, Augur and the men of his division waited in perfect battle order for the signal from General Banks to attack. Banks in turn waited for the sound of Sherman's attack before giving the signal to Augur. Unfortunately, Sherman was having lunch in his tent and passing the time of day with his staff officers.[33]

Sherman was opposed to the attack on the grounds that it was "worse than folly" and would not succeed.[34] He was also apparently in doubt about the decision of the council held the night before. According to Lieutenant Colonel Richard B. Irwin, Sherman may have "supposed he was to wait for the engineers to indicate the point of attack, and . . . did not choose to go beyond what he conceived to be his orders to precipitate a movement whose propriety he doubted." [35] Sherman may simply have been confused by the whole situation, as apparently everyone else was—from Banks on down. It is even possible that Sherman thought he was not supposed to attack.

At 9 A.M. Augur sent Captain Godfrey with two troops of the First Louisiana Cavalry out to establish communications with Sherman, but the troopers were shelled by Confederate batteries and driven back.[36] Agitated by Sherman's inactivity, Banks went galloping over to his headquarters, and, according to Colonel Irwin, "hot words passed" between the two men.[37] Highly incensed by the failure of the West Pointer to act, Banks returned to headquarters determined to replace Sherman with General George L. Andrews. Communications were poor, however, and it was 1:30 P.M. before Andrews reached Sherman's division, where he found the troops drawn up in order of battle and preparing to attack. Andrews generously declined to relay the removal order to Sherman and merely acted as a witness to the great assault.

Union artillery had raked General Beall's line since just after dawn. The 20-pound and 30-pound Parrotts of the First Indiana Heavy Artillery and the lighter field pieces of a multitude of field batteries had scorched the Confederate lines with solid shot, high explosives, and case shot. Many of Beall's guns were disabled, and some Confederates were cut down by the hail of fire. Beall's artillery was able to make only a feeble reply to the vastly overwhelming Union fire, but one gun of Holcomb's Second Vermont Battery was disabled and several Union soldiers wounded.[38] Beall had weakened his line in order to send troops to support Colonel Steedman, and it was not until about 2 P.M. that Miles' Legion, which had been on the Confederate right, moved to the left in order to reinforce Beall's right against Sherman.[39]

As Sherman's troops deployed in line of battle and prepared for the advance across the deadly open ground, Union field batteries began moving up to shorten the range, in order to rake the Confederates with anti-personnel ammunition. In the interval of time between the end of Grover's, Paine's, and Weitzel's attack and the beginning of Sherman's and Augur's advance, at least some of the Confederate troops had pulled back from the left to the center, and more troops arrived during the fighting. The Twenty-third Arkansas, which had been fighting at the Bull Pen that morning, was shifted to Beall's right just in time to help fight off Sherman's advance.[40]

Confederate skirmishers were blasted back behind their breastworks and the way was prepared for the big assault. The First Vermont Battery moved out of the sheltering woods and unlimbered within five hundred yards of the Confederate breastworks.[41]

At 2:15 P.M. Sherman gave the order for the advance to begin. Accompanied by his staff and escort, he led the way across Slaughter's Field, located in the interval between General F. S. Nickerson's brigade on his right and General Neal Dow's brigade on his left. About five hundred yards of comparatively open ground separated the Federals from the Confederate breastworks. Numerous felled trees studded the fields over which the Federals had to pass, and there were three fences which had not been blown down by artillery fire. The fields were intersected by a deep gully, over which the Federals had to cross under heavy fire.[42]

Three hundred colored pioneers, under Captain Joseph Bailey, Fourth Wisconsin, led the attack without weapons but carrying long poles and planks with which to breach the ditch.[43] The volunteer storming party, or "forlorn hope," of Dow's brigade,

130 men commanded by Captain Henry Stark, Sixth Michigan, followed close behind the colored troops. The brigade proper was formed in line of regiments: Sixth Michigan, Colonel Thomas S. Clark; Fifteenth New Hampshire, Colonel John W. Kingman, forming the second line; Twenty-sixth Connecticut, Colonel Thomas Kingsley, in the third line; One Hundred Twenty-eighth New York, Colonel David S. Cowles, bringing up the rear. Companies A and C of the One Hundred Twenty-eighth New York were already engaged with the Confederates as skirmishers. On Sherman's right Nickerson moved forward, his brigade also arranged in lines of regiments. The Fourteenth Maine led his advance, forming an advanced skirmish line. The Twenty-fourth Maine was second in order, the One Hundred Seventy-seventh New York immediately behind it. The One Hundred Sixty-fifth New York, sometimes referred to as Smith's Zouaves, brought up the rear. As Sherman's two brigades moved out from the woods into the open plain, Nickerson's right flank rested on the road running past Slaughter's house; Dow's left advanced along a line near the Gibbon house.[44]

Beall's men greeted the advancing Yankees with tremendous blasts of artillery fire. "Smoking a squatty little pipe" and wearing a smashed-in cap, Captain George Abbay, commanding Company K (Battery K), First Mississippi Field Artillery Regiment, turned to his men and said, "Now boys, I want you to stick to the pieces and give the Yankees hell." [45]

The Federals continued to move forward. General Dow's First Brigade thrust across the field through the young corn and into the entangled mass of the abatis. In crossing the three fences which traversed the plain, the First Brigade was thrown into great confusion. The colored pioneers dropped their burdens and headed for the rear, leaving the white troops to get across the ditch as best they could.[46]

General Sherman was among the first to fall—struck in the right leg by a grapeshot ball, which shattered the bone. His horse was also killed from the same discharge, and his staff was cut to pieces, two men being killed and another wounded. Troops from the Fifteenth New Hampshire carried Sherman to safety; his last order was, "Lead them ahead, straight ahead, dead on the enemy's works." [47] Federal surgeons worked on the general in an open field near the firing line. "They pulled out the loose pieces of bone with pincers, taking hold and yanking at every end that showed. Then they ran their fingers in and felt for more. Finally they stuffed it full of cotton to stop the blood and then bound it up with long strips of muslin." [48] Sherman was taken to New Orleans, where his leg was amputated at the Sisters' Hospital.

With Confederate bullets kicking up dust on the dry ground, General Dow and his men moved forward on the double-quick. When about three hundred yards from the position held by the Twelfth Arkansas Infantry, commanded by Colonel T. G. Reid, Dow was struck in the arm by a spent slug, and seconds later by another, which tore through his left thigh.[49]

With Sherman out of action, Dow became divisional commander. But before he was even cognizant of this fact he was struck down; thus, the command evolved upon General Nickerson. However, in the excitement no one thought to tell him; consequently, the Second Division was left without a commander in the middle of the battle. Even without a leader, Dow's "forlorn hope" advanced close enough to the breastworks to pick off unwary Confederate gunners. The little band was finally forced to take shelter in a nearby ravine, where they lay until dark before they retired to the safety of their own works. Firing buckshot and ball, and double charges of canister, the Confederates broke the charge of the rest of Dow's brigade, but the Yankees rallied and charged again, only to be driven back with heavy losses.[50]

The scene in front of the Confederate works was one of pandemonium. Exploding shells started many fires among the abatis. Yankee soldiers were shot down by the dozens as they attempted to scramble over the felled trees and sharpened limbs which protected the Confederate works. Colonel Cowles of the One Hundred Twenty-eighth New York was bayoneted as he tried to force his way inside the Confederate earthworks, and died in agony half an hour later.[51]

The attack of the First Brigade was a failure, and the battered survivors took shelter where they could. Many headed for the woods five hundred yards in the rear from which they had originally set out; others took shelter at the bottom of the gully.

The advance of Nickerson's brigade was somewhat slower than that of Dow's. The One Hundred Sixty-fifth New York, which had been in the rear of the brigade, shifted to the left and began a rapid forward movement on a line oblique to the rest of the brigade.[52] The Zouaves charged across Slaughter's Field in line of battle, their red breeches and caps presenting fine targets to the Confederate sharpshooters. Southern gunners slashed the New Yorkers with spherical case shot and, as the range closed, with grape, and finally with double loads of canister. At a range of 150 yards the Confederate infantry were ordered to fire, and they raked the Zouaves with buck and ball. Their ranks ripped into shreds by the murderous fire, the Zouaves wavered and finally stopped. Lieutenant Colonel Abel Smith, Jr., ordered his surviving Zouaves to take cover on the ground. Smith set an example for courage by walking back and forth among his men as calmly as though he were on a parade ground.[53] Soon Smith fell, mortally wounded, and then his second in command, Major Gouverneur Carr, was shot down. The Zouaves finally broke under the terrible pounding they were sustaining. Although some fled in panic, many of the New Yorkers took cover behind stumps, logs, or rough ground, and started sniping. Meanwhile, the Zouaves' colors were lying on the battlefield about seventy yards from the breastworks. The sight of the colors lying there was too much for a Louisiana Confederate named Clark, who was about fifteen or sixteen years old. He started to dash out toward the temptation, but was stopped by Captain Robert L. Pruyn's shout, "Here, you, boy, you'll be killed out there! and then what will your mother say?" In the meantime, another young Confederate, Matt Howley, also of the Fourth Louisiana, dashed out and picked up the flag, returning to the inside of the breastworks with the fine trophy. "There, now," young Clark said with indignation, "Matt's got the flag, and he didn't get killed either." [54]

Even as the Zouaves broke, the rest of Nickerson's brigade

charged forward. Covered by the fire of the sharpshooting Zouaves, the New York and Maine volunteers drove to within a
hundred yards of Beall's line before faltering.[55] Nickerson's officers and some of his men tried to persuade the waverers to attack
again but without success, and the Confederates emitted loud
cheers as the brigade finally broke and fled to the rear. As on
other parts of Slaughter's Field, artillery fire had ignited the
trees and brush, and the Federals had great difficulty carrying
away their wounded in order to keep them from being burned
alive.[56]

In a clump of woods Nickerson's brigade was finally rallied
and made a second charge with an even smaller measure of
success. Many of Nickerson's men drifted into a ravine on the
right to get some cover from the devastatingly accurate Confederate fire. The men of both Dow and Nickerson had fought
bravely, but they had met with a major reverse. It was up to
General Christopher Augur to capture Port Hudson—if it were
to be done at all.

As soon as Banks heard the noise of Sherman's advance, he
ordered Augur forward. Augur's dispositions were simple. Colonel Chapin's brigade, which was deployed along the Plains Store
road, was to make the actual assault; Colonel Dudley's brigade
was to be held in reserve on the right of the road. Chapin deployed part of the Twenty-first Maine to cover his advance by
acting as skirmishers. The storming column—two hundred men
under Lieutenant Colonel James O'Brien, Forty-eighth Massachusetts—occupied the point of the woods on the left of the
Plains Store road. The Forty-ninth Massachusetts was behind
them. With the Forty-eighth, the Second Louisiana (Dudley's
brigade) and the remainder of the Twenty-first Maine supporting
the Forty-ninth Massachusetts, the One Hundred Sixteenth New
York was deployed on the right of the road.[57] In addition to
the Second Louisiana Infantry, Dudley had the One Hundred
Sixty-first New York, the One Hundred Seventy-fourth New
York, the Thirtieth Massachusetts, and the Fiftieth Massachusetts in reserve. To support Chapin's advance, Augur had in position eight 30-pound Parrotts and one battery of 20-pound Par-

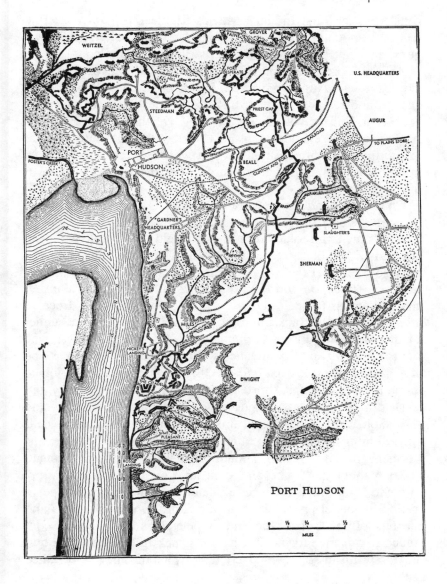

PORT HUDSON

0   ½   ¼   ½
MILES

rotts from the First Indiana, Mack's Eighteenth New York Battery of 20-pound Parrotts, the Second Vermont Battery of Sawyer guns, and the Fourth Massachusetts Battery (Napoleons).[58]

As the skirmishers of the Twenty-first Maine engaged the Confederates, Augur gave the following order: "Now, boys, charge, and reserve your fire till you get into the fort; give them cold steel, and as you charge cheer! Give them New England! A Connecticut regiment is inside, but they have exhausted their ammunition. In fifteen minutes you will be there. Press on, no matter who may fall. If ten men get over the walls, the place is ours." [59]

Chapin's brigade surged forward, and O'Brien called out to his men, "Come boys! Pick up your bundles and follow me." [60] Chapin's men had to advance across a field a half mile wide and covered with fallen trees which acted as barriers. The obstacles were so thick that the Federal field officers had to dismount and lead the attack on foot. With whoops and yells, the Yankees charged across the field against a murderously hot fire. Located in a redan at the Jackson road, a group of Alabamans under Lieutenant John Frank, Company K, First Alabama, sighted "The Baby" in on the advancing Union line, slamming round after round of explosives into it. Other Confederate guns joined in, and as the range shortened the Confederate infantry unleashed a furious blast of musketry. Screams of "I am hit!" and "Oh God, I'm killed" rang amid the sound of bursting shells and whining shrapnel.[61] Laden with their heavy bundles, the stormers began to lag behind. Hysterical with excitement, O'Brien shouted, "Come on, boys; we'll wash in the Mississippi to-night." [62] Minutes later he fell dead, a Confederate slug penetrating his bullet-proof vest.[63] In the confusion the stormers and the rest of the brigade became hopelessly mixed up and continued to advance together. Chapin, struck in the face by a bullet, threw up his hands and cried, "My God! They have killed me." [64]

Even as the Federals began to falter, one-legged Colonel William Bartlett, the only Yankee on the battlefield astride a horse, galloped straight toward the Confederate lines, his steed surmounting the obstacles with apparent ease. A bullet struck Bartlett in his foot, and another shattered his left wrist. He lost his balance and fell to the ground, and his horse Billy galloped to the rear. When a soldier ran up to help Bartlett, the colonel immediately exclaimed, "Did you see Billy? He jumped like a rabbit." [65]

Their assault having failed, many of the Federals took cover behind the stumps and logs in front of the Confederate works and began sniping. The Second Louisiana came charging up the Plains Store road, but too late to help, as Chapin's brigade had been stopped already. Although Confederate losses in repulsing Chapin's attack were light, the artillery suffered severely from sniper fire. Indeed, the crew of "The Baby" was almost annihilated. While ramming a charge home, Private Henry Smith was picked off by a sniper. He died in agony six weeks later, July 10, the day after the surrender of the Port.[66] Corporal J. A. Fergerson stepped into Private Smith's place and was shot down; he died that night. Private J. Hayes soon dropped to the ground severely wounded, leaving only Lieutenant John Frank, Jr. and Sergeant W. L. Ellis to man "The Baby." The two men fired several rounds at the Federals before Frank fell, wounded by a Minié ball. Sergeant Ellis carried the wounded officer to General Beall's headquarters and gave him water from Beall's canteen, but Frank died that night.[67]

The crew of "The Baby" and the other Confederates who had fallen had not been struck down in vain, for Augur's advance was completely halted. Banks was ready to throw the remainder of Dudley's brigade in when the news of Sherman's repulse arrived. He decided to call it a day.

Although the battle was over, many hundreds of Union soldiers were still isolated out on the field of battle, pinned down by Confederate fire. To evacuate these men safely, several Federal officers had flags of truce raised. The Confederates then ceased firing, whereupon the trapped Yankees scrambled back to the safety of their own lines. The last fighting of the day took place when a party of Federals, under a white flag, attempted to rush a portion of the Confederate right. They were soon repulsed.[68]

The fighting which had begun around 6 A.M. was over by 6 P.M., and it only remained for both sides to count the cost. Confederate losses were never exactly determined, but ran around 250 to 275 killed, wounded, and missing. Most of the casualties occurred in Steedman's command.[69] According to Banks's report, Union losses on May 27 were 293 killed, 1,545 wounded, and 157 missing. Most of the missing were probably killed, and many of the wounded died.[70] Although the proportion of casualties to troops involved in the assault of May 27 was low, some of the individual regiments suffered losses fully equal to those of units engaged at Antietam, Gettysburg, and Second Manassas. The troops engaged in the assault suffered about 10 per cent casualties as compared to 16 per cent losses for the Union army at Perryville and 13 per cent casualties at Chancellorsville. The Zouave regiment had 15 killed, 80 wounded, and 3 missing. The Eighth New Hampshire Infantry was the most chopped-up Union regiment. Two hundred and ninety-eight men had moved forward early that morning for an attack on the Tenth Arkansas, and of this number 124 were shot down, a loss of 41 per cent for the New Hampshire troops. Even the Union regiments which were not closely engaged were badly cut up by Confederate sharpshooters. The Fifty-third Massachusetts lost 30 men killed, wounded, and missing, while merely engaged in sniping. The hardest hit Confederate regiment was Colonel Ben Johnson's Fifteenth Arkansas, which lost 76 men on May 27. The First Alabama lost 75 men, and the Tenth Arkansas lost nearly 80. Most of the other Confederate regiments escaped with only 2 or 3 casualties, although hotly engaged.[71]

The majority of Federal regiments were blooded that day, but many suffered less than a dozen casualties. For twelve hours of fighting, the Union Army of the Gulf gained a few yards of ground and wrecked a few Confederate cannon. Port Hudson should have fallen, but it did not. Upon whom should the blame be placed? Banks blamed everybody and everything from his superiors to the Confederate defenses. He stated that the works were "impregnable."[72] His early morning boast that "Port Hudson will be ours today"[73] degenerated into the mournful post-

May 27 cry, "My force is too weak for the work it has to do." [74]
Banks howled, "General Sherman has failed utterly and crimi-
nally to bring his men into the field." [75]

From Augur's headquarters came a different and more realistic
analysis of the failure:

The bloody results of that day taught us what the people of the
North are not always ready to believe, namely, that it is far easier
to talk of taking a strongly-fortified place than to do it, and our brave
fellows are now paying the dear penalty of that insane supineness which
ever permitted such a fortress as Port Hudson to be built, when we
could at one time have prevented it with scarcely more than a corporal's guard. [76]

Blaming his superiors and subordinates, Banks did not seem
to realize that the ultimate success or failure of an army rests on
its commander. The Union soldiers paid a dear price in blood
for the indecision and incompetence of the Union high command.

VIII

Spade and Cannon

THE bloody assault of May 27, 1863, was over. The Union forces had pounded hard at the Southerners, but had failed to make any appreciable gap in their defenses. Shocked by their defeat, the soldiers of Banks's army paused to stare and wonder at this semi-circular-shaped section of Louisiana which had halted their mighty blue columns. Port Hudson and the surrounding countryside did not bear the look of a place of slaughter. The gently sloping land was covered by deserted plantations and beautiful groves of magnolias and hardwoods. Many brooks and streams crisscrossed the land, making a perplexing network of ravines and valleys, the latter of which were "heavily timbered and choked with underbrush." [1]

All through the long day of May 27 Farragut's fleet had poured in flame, metal, and death on the defenders of the Port, with the Southerners able to make but a feeble reply. On the morning following the assault the Confederates lashed back furiously in a desperate attempt to even the score. Gunners from Company K, First Alabama, and from De Gournay's battalion were ordered to take the 30-pound Parrott rifle and an old rifled 24-pounder down to the formerly abandoned Battery No. XI for a try at the Union fleet. The road to the isolated battery had been badly torn up by Yankee gunfire, and it was nearly dawn before the Louisianians and Alabamans reached the isolated gun position with their two weapons. Battery No. XI had been designed to hold one gun, and the parapet was only about three feet high, but by about 6 A.M. the guns were in position and ready to fire. Lieutenant M. E. Pratt, commanding the little force, gave the order that opened the engagement. The two guns splattered the *Essex,* anchored a

68

mile or more distant, and the ironclad soon returned the fire. Within ten minutes every ship in the Union fleet, including the six mortar boats, had opened up on the Southerners with a tremendous rain of explosives.

A 9-inch shell knocked off a canteen that had been hanging on the knob of the cascabel of the Parrott and wounded Private Josiah Tunnell. Flung to the ground by the impact of the shell, Tunnell suddenly jumped up, wiped the dirt off his face, and exclaimed, "Well, boys they liked to have got me." [2] Lieutenant Pratt was the next to fall under the murderous Union fire. While he was on the parapet directing the fire of the gun, a shell exploded just below his feet, hurling him into the battery with wounds in his hand and hip. One of De Gournay's men was also wounded, but the *Essex* was forced to fall back out of range, and the *Genesee* was also severely damaged. After firing ninety-nine rounds, the Confederates broke off the fight.

Even while Pratt and his men were slashing at Farragut's fleet, Banks was preparing to settle down to a formal siege. Provisions were made for ammunition and other supplies to be brought up, and Banks established new headquarters in the rear of the center of the Union lines. [3] During the morning of the twenty-eighth he requested a flag of truce from General Gardner in order to remove the dead and wounded still lying sprawled on the battlefield. After the previous day's experience with Yankee flags of truce, the Confederates were a bit shy about accepting this new Northern proposal, but finally agreed to the truce on humanitarian grounds. [4]

The Confederates' lack of confidence proved justifiable, for while the truce was in force, hundreds of Northern soldiers worked at constructing fortifications in advanced positions on the battlefield. Many Union soldiers who had been exposed to Confederate fire before the truce was declared were in well protected positions from which they could snipe at the Southerners when the truce ended. [5] Oddly enough, while the truce was in effect, many of the blue and gray mingled on the battlefield, exchanging coffee, tobacco, bread, souvenirs, and stories of close escapes. [6]

The truce expired at 7 P.M., but as there were still Union

soldiers who had not been brought in, the Confederates did not molest the stretcher-bearers. Finally the last Yanks were carried off at 7:30 P.M. Expecting the Confederates to be relaxed as a result of the truce, the Yankees made a furious attack on the First Alabama Infantry, and the battle raged for an hour; however, the Yankees were finally repulsed.[7]

General Richard Arnold was instructed to bring up the remainder of the siege train, and Major D. C. Houston was ordered to provide entrenching tools and siege materials. The Union siege artillery numbered forty pieces, ranging from 24-pound rifles to 13-inch mortars. Banks's field artillery numbered between sixty and ninety-two guns, mostly modern rifles, with a large number of Napoleons. To this formidable armament was added the powerful batteries of Farragut's warships. To combat the Union artillery, General Gardner's little army had fifty-one guns, many light 6-pounders, and most of the others obsolete models. The Confederate garrison was somewhat outgunned—roughly ten to one.[8]

To bolster their fighting strength, the Yankees brought in strong troop reinforcements. On May 28 the Union garrison at Brashear City received the following message: "There is severe fighting up the river. Forward at once all the troops that can be spared."[9] The Forty-first Massachusetts (Third Massachusetts Cavalry), One Hundred Fourteenth New York, Fourth Massachusetts, Sixteenth New Hampshire, Twenty-second Maine, Ninetieth New York, Fifty-second Massachusetts, Twenty-sixth Maine regiments, and a detachment of the Thirteenth Connecticut were brought to Port Hudson by steamer between May 28 and June 1.[10] Although additional reinforcements arrived later, the effective fighting strength of Banks's army was probably greatest on or about June 1—25,000 to 27,000 men.

While the Federals were engaged in bringing up artillery and fresh troops, Gardner's men were making preparations to defend the Port. Zones were set up along the defense perimeter, and engineer officers were put in charge of each. Lieutenant Stork was placed in command of the river line and extreme right. Lieutenant James Freret was assigned the line of land fortifications, and

Lieutenant Fred Y. Dabney took over the left wing. The top of the parapet was loopholed, in some places with sandbags, and in others with earth. The 10-inch gun disabled on May 26 was repaired and was ready for service on May 29.[11]

The enemy's fire grew increasingly annoying. Along the southern line of defenses the Yankees planted an 8-inch howitzer which they fired with reduced charges. The shells from this gun, named "Bounding Bet" by the Confederates,[12] would ricochet along the ground, skipping and bouncing along, and finally roll "as slowly as a ball in a bowling alley" before exploding.[13] One of "Bounding Bet's" projectiles which failed to explode was opened and was found to contain 480 copper balls. If the gun's fire was something less than deadly, that of the other enemy batteries had a strong effect on the Confederates. "Confederate artillery could not fire a gun without having the fire of a dozen pieces concentrated on it. . . . Finally the artillerists were compelled to withdraw their guns from the batteries and only run them in when a charge was made." [14] The guns were placed in pits in the rear of the gun platforms, where they were comparatively safe from enemy fire. To offset the superior Union artillery fire, Colonel Marshall J. Smith, Confederate Chief of Artillery, had the 10-inch Columbiad in Battery No. IV turned around to bear on the Union army batteries.[15] The Southerners mounted the big gun on a railroad car, enabling them to shift the gun's position up and down the railroad track.[16] The Yankee soldiers who were bombarded with this ponderous weapon christened the gun "The Lady Davis" and "The Demoralizer." Whenever De Gournay's men fired the mighty gun, the air was rent by strange and terrible shrieking sounds, for the Confederates were short of regulation ammunition and were using anything they could cram down the muzzle of "The Lady," from flat irons to nails.

The Port Hudson garrison had a fairly good supply of powder,[17] but was short on projectiles for most of the fifty-one guns. Even during the great assault of May 27, the Southerners had found it necessary to use homemade cannon ammunition. The Confederates would "cut off the sleeves of their shirts and underclothing," tie up one end, and fill the improvised bags with slugs and scraps of iron.[18] The bags were then rammed home in the cannon and discharged at the enemy, spraying him with cane knives, railroad spikes, bolts, hatchets, ramrods, nuts, wooden plugs fastened together with cotton, and broken pieces of bayonets.[19] A lack of projectiles was not the Confederates' only problem, for one by one their cannon were smashed or disabled by Federal fire. The fire from the Union fleet was especially destructive to their artillery. The rifled 32-pounder in Battery No. X was temporarily disabled on June 5, and on June 11 the 24-pound rifle in Battery No. XI was knocked out. All of the batteries were brought under fire, and several men killed or wounded. But the worst disaster took place on June 12, when De Gournay's fine 30-pound Parrott took three successive direct hits and was reduced to scrap metal.[20]

General Banks and Admiral Farragut maintained close communication concerning the bombardment. Union navy gunners made repeated attempts to explode the main Confederate magazine, which was reported by Banks to be "behind battery No. 6, and from 300 to 500 yards back from the river." [21] The mortar boats opened up a hot fire in the reported vicinity of the magazine, but they failed to score any hits. Banks reported that beef cattle had been killed, several soldiers wounded, and a "regimental camp rendered untenable" from the effects of the mortar fire.[22] The gunboats continued to spray Port Hudson with explosives, causing the Confederates to burrow into the ground like moles.

The men of the Fourth Louisiana were especially troubled by the fire from the *Genesee's* big gun. In desperation they constructed a magnificent bombproof which was affectionately called "the gopher hole." [23] This place of refuge was a hole in the ground about fifteen feet deep and ten or twelve feet square, roofed with logs and covered with several inches of earth. In this refuge the Louisianians were safe from anything but a direct hit, although exploding shells did spatter the entrance with great "gobs" of black mud.

Yankee sniping was another hazard to the Confederates. With their good Springfields and Enfields, Banks's snipers could pick off men at points three hundred to four hundred yards inside the Confederate breastworks.[24] Inside Port Hudson no man dared walk upright near the breastworks for fear a slug would strike him down. Major James T. Coleman's battalion of Miles' Legion, which had temporarily relieved the First Alabama on the Confederate left, was particularly pestered by Northern snipers. On June 3 Major Coleman had one man killed and five wounded from sniper fire in a matter of hours.[25]

The hot Louisiana sun took its toll of Confederates. "Exhausted by long hours on duty, the men would frequently fall asleep at their posts, and after the fierce rays of the sun had beat down on them for an hour or so they would wake up delirious. Some fell asleep in the sun and never awoke again." [26] The heat caused some of the Confederates to erect "shebangs" in the rear of the breastworks. These were actually crude tents erected by means of a blanket covering a ridge pole, with stakes driven into the ground to hold the corners of the blanket out. Privates Edward Young McMorries and Newton Soles of the First Alabama erected a shebang on a hillside on which breastworks had been constructed. Soles walked over to slip under the tent and for a second his head showed above the edge of the breastworks. A single rifle cracked, and he rolled down the hill into a ditch, a bullet through his head.[27]

Death was always lurking near the defenders of Port Hudson. In an attempt to relieve the tension, the Southerners resorted to various amusements, including cards and checkers. While engaging in a friendly game of checkers, one soldier thought his opponent was taking an unusually long time to move. Becoming impatient, he irritably inquired why. Then he saw that the other player had been killed by a sniper's slug, which had not even jolted the body over.[28] The attrition of war was taking a heavy toll of the already pitifully few defenders of Port Hudson. Life in the river stronghold was dirty, rough, and dangerous, but rarely dull. One Confederate soldier, sitting in a trench in front of the Twelfth Connecticut Infantry, received a horrible shock as a sputtering 8-inch mortar shell suddenly landed beside him. Prodded into action by the sight of the flickering fuse, the soldier went flying over the front of the parapet. The shell exploded with a thunderous roar, gouging a great chunk out of the ground. As the smoke cleared, the quick-thinking Rebel dived back over the parapet. Delighted by the display of ingenuity and agility, the men of the Twelfth Connecticut cheered the "Johnny" instead of shooting at him.[29]

Behind their own breastworks the Union soldiers had their share of dangerous adventures. Confederate sharpshooters constantly made things interesting for those Yanks who chose to move carelessly about behind their parapets. Many officers were picked off by Confederate sharpshooters. Lieutenant George W. Thompson of the already battered Eighth New Hampshire was killed in the rifle pits on May 29.[30] While engaging in a spot of sharpshooting, Lieutenant Louis Beckwith of the Thirteenth Connecticut had a toe shot away by a Confederate sharpshooter, causing Beckwith to engage in language not exactly suitable for an officer and gentleman.[31] During pay call the men of the Twelfth Connecticut suddenly found themselves under fire from one of their own Napoleon batteries. The troops stood rigidly at attention while the last man was paid off and then shouldered arms, faced to the right, ported arms, broke ranks, and headed for cover. The incident had a happy ending, however, for the only casualty was the regimental coward of the One Hundred Fourteenth New York, "who had shirked every fight, and who had dug himself a gopher-hole unattainable by the fire of the garrison. The second ball found him out in his retreat, took off a leg and sent him into the other world." [32] Cowards being looked upon with disfavor in the army, one Yankee soldier "offered to show the commandant of the battery two or three more gopher-holes which he thought ought to be cleaned out." [33]

The Union army at Port Hudson faced one unique problem which their descendants on Guadalcanal seventy-nine years later ran into—tree sniping. The tall cypress trees, heavily clad with Spanish moss, made excellent perches for Confederate sharpshooters. At night the Southerners climbed forty or fifty feet up the trees, covered themselves with moss, and waited for dawn. Any Yankee soldier who dared move was likely to get a slug through his head. One Confederate, armed with a heavy double-barrelled shotgun of English make which fired ounce and a half slugs, picked off Northerners at ranges of almost a mile. The Federals could not spot the tree in which the Rebel sharpshooter was stationed, although they tried.[34] Captain John L. Barstow's manservant had a cup of coffee knocked out of his hand by a rifle slug, and Lieutenant Colonel Charles Dillingham, Eighth Vermont, had the top of his tent carried off by a cannon ball while he was inside it. Miraculously, he escaped injury.[35]

Disregarding all hazards, the Yankees continued to advance their works toward those of the Southerners, employing the complicated techniques of siege warfare primarily evolved from the maxims of Marshal Vauban, but strongly modified by the lessons learned at the siege of Sevastopol during the Crimean War. Vauban's system was based on the gradual advance of siege artillery from extreme range to a point from where it could fire point-blank at the enemy works and breach them. In order to advance the guns, Vauban relied on covering artillery fire and on the construction of trenches in which infantry was stationed to protect the advanced batteries from sorties by the defending enemy troops. The trenches formed a succession of parallels which gradually closed in on the enemy works. Once the parallels were close enough and the advanced batteries established, the garrison of the besieged place could be bombarded into submission or taken by storm through breaches in their works made by the besiegers' artillery.

At Port Hudson the Federals followed Vauban's ideas, but used their improved artillery for indirect fire from greater ranges than conceived of by the Frenchman. The Union infantrymen pushed cotton bales forward, behind which the work of digging trenches was commenced, with black troops responsible for most of the digging and carpentry. Batteries were gradually thrown up behind the cotton bales, protected by strong parapets with embrasures, plank platforms, and magazines. The guns were then wheeled into position by the artillerymen. On one occasion when the colored pioneers were suddenly seized with panic and headed for the rear, the white troops acting as their support, supposing the Confederates to be attacking, cocked their rifles and got ready for a desperate fight. No Confederates materialized, however. One Union soldier, Sergeant Solomon Nelson of the Fiftieth Massachusetts, wryly wrote in his diary: "These colored soldiers are said to fight nobly; we know that they are great on backward advances; they will beat the world on making charges to the rear." [36] The white Union troops were not immune to panic. On the night of June 7 a soldier of the Forty-eighth Massachusetts had a nightmare and knocked over a stack of rifles. Believing themselves attacked, the entire regiment turned out, ready to fight the Rebels to the death, and it was some time before order was restored.[37]

While Union and Confederate gunners and sharpshooters traded shots, the Union Army of the Gulf (Nineteenth Army Corps), underwent a major shake-up. The heavy officer casualties of May 27 made reorganization necessary. General Nickerson, who had assumed command of T. W. Sherman's division on May 27, was reduced to brigade command, and his place filled by General William Dwight. Although slightly wounded, Neal Dow hoped to assume command of the Second Division. When Dwight was given the command, Dow attempted to obtain a transfer from the Department of the Gulf; but Banks refused to let him go, even after giving Colonel Thomas Clark command of Dwight's old brigade.[38] Colonel Charles J. Paine assumed command of Colonel Chapin's old brigade. Along with the various changes in command, positional changes for the infantry and artillery units occurred. General Halbert Paine's division was shifted from Grover's right flank to his left, in a position to cover the Jackson road. Grover assumed command of the whole right wing. The left wing was placed under the direction of General Augur. The various commands were moved about to form a solid wall of blue around Port Hudson.

The completion of reorganization allowed Banks to devote some time to the problem of disposing of the little cavalry force —commanded by Colonel John Logan—which was lurking in the rear of the Army of the Gulf. Colonel Grierson, commanding Union cavalry at Port Hudson, was given the task of disposing of the pestiferous Logan. On the morning of June 3 Grierson received word that Logan's cavalry was at Clinton. At 5 A.M. he and about 1,300 troops, supported by eight cannon, left for a raid on the town.[39]

Perceiving Grierson's advance, Colonel Stockdale and his battalion ambushed the Yankee raiders a short distance from Clinton, while dispatching a trooper to warn Colonel Logan. Logan was engaged in a poker game with Colonels Griffith and Powers when Stockdale's messenger arrived. He immediately ordered his bugler to sound "Boots and Saddles," and within minutes the Confederates were galloping to the rescue of the hard-pressed Mississippians, who had been pushed back to Pretty Creek. Logan sent Colonel Powers to outflank Grierson while he attacked head-on. The Yankees were badly cut up and Grierson was forced to retreat to Port Hudson, his rear guard under heavy attack. His losses were eight killed, twenty-eight wounded, and fifteen captured; Logan suffered but twenty casualties.[40]

Irritated by Grierson's defeat, Banks dispatched General Paine, with a powerful force of artillery, infantry, and cavalry, to crush Logan. Leaving Port Hudson on June 5, the Yankees took two days to reach Clinton. They captured twenty sick and wounded Confederates. The only Union casualties were several score infantrymen who collapsed from sunstroke or from drinking too much captured Louisiana rum.[41]

After the failure of Grierson's expedition, Banks decided to direct his attention toward a speedy reduction of the Port Hudson garrison. Hopelessly outgunned, the Southerners rarely used their cannon any more, saving them for the big assault they expected to come. In an effort to locate the Confederate batteries, Banks launched an armed reconnaissance against the Port early on the morning of June 11. In the words of Lieutenant Colonel Richard B. Irwin, the expedition was for the purpose "of harassing the enemy, of inducing him to bring forward and expose his artillery, acquiring a knowledge before the enemy's front, and of favoring the operations of pioneers who may be sent forward to remove obstructions if necessary." [42]

Banks's decision to launch the expedition turned the morning of June 11 into a time of terror for the Federal soldiers. Godfrey Weitzel's and Joseph S. Morgan's brigades were thrown forward in a tragic comedy of errors. There were blunders in transmitting orders to the regiments involved, and the Union attack was soon broken up. Caught in the open by Confederate fire, the Federals endured the leaden hail for a while, when a sudden thunderstorm burst overhead. For a brief hour the firing gave way before "the torrents of a grateful and less destructive rain." [43] Soon after the storm subsided, hostilities were resumed and the Federals returned to their own lines as best they could. Many Union soldiers were captured in the attack after wandering into the Confederate lines. The total casualty list was heavy. Two of Weitzel's men were killed, forty-one wounded, and six captured; Morgan lost seventy-one wounded or missing, although some of those missing eventually made their way back to Union lines. Casualties in other units were not reported. The only thing gained was that two Confederate cannon, which had raked the attacking Yanks with grapeshot, were soon disabled by Union artillery fire. [44]

Although Banks's armed reconnaissance had turned into a minor disaster, inside Port Hudson conditions were rapidly deteriorating. Food and ammunition were running short, and the strain was beginning to tell on the men. General Gardner felt that it was of the utmost importance to enter into communications with General Joseph E. Johnston. Since the siege had begun, Gardner had sent numerous messengers to his superior in Mississippi, but all had been either killed or captured. On June 11 Gardner decided to send Captain Robert L. Pruyn of the Fourth Louisiana. The message Pruyn carried was, "I have repulsed the enemy in several attacks but am still closely invested. I am getting short of provisions and ammunition of all kinds and should be speedily reinforced." [45]

At 9:30 P.M. Pruyn slipped into muddy waters of the Mississippi River, clad in civilian clothes and held up by a crude raft made of empty canteens. He swam downriver through the enemy's patrols and finally passed through the Federal fleet. Swimming by the *Genesee*, he was spotted by a crewman, but escaped without injury and eventually landed on the west bank at dawn—nine miles below Port Hudson. Sympathizers provided Pruyn with a boat, and he crossed the river and eventually reached Johnston's headquarters in Jackson. The general read the dispatch and gave Pruyn a message to deliver to Gardner, whereupon Pruyn began the long trip back. After many dangerous experiences, he reached Port Hudson and delivered his message.[46]

Even while Pruyn was making his dangerous journey through Union lines, Banks was preparing for what he felt was to be the final assault. At 11:15 A.M., June 13, the Federals opened up with every gun and mortar they had. Shells fell at the rate of more than one a second. The Confederates could not fight back, and could only lie in their trenches and endure the terrible crescendo of explosions. After an hour the bombardment ended. As silence settled over Port Hudson, the Union forces exhibited a flag of truce, and a message was delivered to General Gardner from Union headquarters. The gist of Banks's missive was that the Southerners were on the verge of starvation, short of ammunition, hopelessly outnumbered, and overwhelmingly outgunned, and that the honorable and sensible course was for Gardner to surrender. Banks hinted that if Gardner did not immediately surrender, the attacking Union army might massacre the Port Hudson garrison if the place were taken by storm.[47]

General Gardner was seated in his office when Banks's message arrived. As he opened and read the dispatch, a smile began to play on his features. He exclaimed to his staff officers, "Ah, Gentlemen!" Then, breaking into a wide grin and stroking his beard, he said, "What do you think? Why Banks has notified me that to avoid unnecessary slaughter he demands the immediate surrender of my forces." [48] Gardner's answer was to order his men to prepare for a fight. His reply to Banks, short and succinct, was, "My duty requires me to defend this position, and therefore I decline to surrender." [49]

Upon receiving Gardner's reply, Banks ordered the artillery to open fire again, and the bombardment recommenced, continuing through the long night. When Grover heard of Gardner's refusal to surrender, he remarked, "Old Gardner was always as obstinate as a mule," to which Weitzel replied, "Well, we know what comes next." [50]

Colonel Thomas S. Clark sent a party of fifty men from the Twenty-sixth Connecticut and fifty men from the Fifteenth New Hampshire to make a demonstration against the Confederate works. The Yankees moved forward as skirmishers, but were soon pinned down by the deadly Confederate fire. The troops managed to withdraw after darkness fell on the battlefield. The Fifteenth New Hampshire lost thirteen killed and wounded in this affair.[51]

In anticipation of the forthcoming attack, Colonel Dudley ordered the Fiftieth Massachusetts to report to General Dwight. Colonel Charles J. Paine detached the Forty-eighth Massachusetts from his command, ordering Colonel Eben F. Stone to report to Dwight. Led by a guide who did not know the way, the regiment got lost and it was nearly morning before Stone reported to Dwight.[52] Dudley was ordered to report to Grover on the right, with the One Hundred Sixty-first and One Hundred Seventy-fourth New York regiments. Before dark on the evening of June 13 Banks and his divisional commanders met at headquarters to make the final plans for the forthcoming attack.

While the bombardment raged during the long night of June 13, a strange phenomenon occurred inside Port Hudson. A tidal wave six feet or more in height rushed up the river, and at the same time Battery No. VI collapsed into the river, one gun being lost beneath the muddy water. What caused the wave and the cave-in was never satisfactorily explained, but it was a strange omen for the next day's bloody occurrences.[53]

By midnight a general assault was agreed on, and it was ordered for early the next morning. The program of action called for Augur to open a heavy fire of artillery on his front, followed in thirty minutes by a feigned attack of skirmishers. Dwight was to take two regiments and try to discover an entrance on the extreme left of the works close to the river. Grover was to make the main attack on the position known as the Priest Cap. The artillery cross-fire was to commence at 3 A.M., but was to cease at a signal given by Grover. At 3:30 A.M. the skirmishers were to attack. "The general formation of each of the two columns of attack had been settled in orders issued from headquarters on the morning of the 11th." [54] Each of the two columns was to be preceded and protected by three hundred skirmishers. Following directly behind the skirmishers, carrying thirty-five axes, ten pickaxes, two hatchets, eighteen shovels, and two handsaws, were to be seventy pioneers. The "forlorn hope," three hundred strong, was to follow the pioneers, each man carrying a bag of cotton. Thirty-four men were to follow, carrying chesses and balks to make a bridge over the ditch. The main assaulting column was to follow next, in lines of battle, with the field artillery and its own pioneers. The cavalry was assigned the job of picketing and guarding the rear, as well as "holding the telegraph road leading out of Port Hudson toward Bayou Sara, by which it was thought the garrison might attempt to escape, on finding their lines broken through, or even to avoid the blow." [55] General Banks was optimistic about the attack.

All watches were set at division and brigade headquarters at nine o'clock by a telegraphic signal, in agreement with the adjutant general's time. The final orders of the anticipated assault bore the hour of 11:30 P.M. Many arrangements were not completed, but things were shaping up for the long-to-be-remembered assault of June 14, 1863.

IX

June 14

ON May 27 Port Hudson had been protected by a mere earth-
work, over which "a fox hunter could have leaped." [1] But in the
eighteen days that had elapsed since the assault the Confederates
had worked diligently in strengthening the works. The knowledge
that their lives might well depend upon it undoubtedly stimulated
them to great exertions. Rifle pits were dug, parapets strength-
ened, and bombproofs constructed. By June 13 the Confederate
works had taken on their permanent shape and character. There
were four principal fronts. The southerly front ran from the
"Citadel" along the crest of the ravine to an angle in front of
General Augur's position. There was a strong detached redan in
front of this line. The second principal front swung off to the left
and ran to the Plains Road—a distance of a mile. The third front
turned slightly to the left and ran from the Plains Road to the
position known as the Priest Cap. The line of works then turned
—running across the head of a ravine—in the direction of Fort
Desperate in front of Grover and Weitzel. These four fronts covered a line some three miles long. From the detached work in
front of Grover and Weitzel to the river there was no continuous
line of works but, rather, a series of rifle pits and dugouts. There
were no enclosed works along the line of landworks, and no interior retrenchments, revetted ditches, or impediments in the
ditches. The works were crude but strong. [2]

In addition to improved fortifications, the Confederates had
also increased their fire power. After the May 27 assault many of
the defenders had crept out into no man's land and gathered up
rifles and ammunition from the fallen "Bluebellies." Following
the armed reconnaissance of June 11 the Southerners captured

more rifles, and by June 13 many of the soldiers on the firing line had two guns—a Union rifle for sharpshooting and a Confederate musket loaded with buckshot for close work.[3] Confederate morale was much improved; the sight of two thousand enemy soldiers lying sprawled on the battlefield on May 27 had done wonders in raising the already high spirits of the Port Hudson defenders. A few faint hearts, mostly foreign or Northern-born conscripts, deserted to Banks's army. The deserters told the Yankees wild tales of starvation and hardships. It is possible that at least some of these deserters were acting under orders from General Gardner, the idea being to convince Banks that Port Hudson would fall if he launched another attack.

In his desire to bring about a quick and decisive end to the siege, Banks began making preparations for another grand assault. Union prospects for a successful assault were good; many Confederate cannon had been wrecked, and the garrison had suffered considerable losses from disease and gunfire. It was 1 A.M. on June 14 before the final orders were circulated among the Union officers. With the attack scheduled to commence at 3:30 A.M., the Federals had but two and a half hours to make all the final arrangements.

At three, Federal artillery opened up with a tremendous barrage. But a thick fog had settled over the entire battlefield, muffling the roar of the big guns. General Paine passed along the front of his regiment, giving final orders for the advance. About 4 A.M. Paine's division commenced its forward movement, the Fourth Wisconsin under Captain Webster P. Moore [4] and the Eighth New Hampshire Infantry under Captain William M. Barrett leading the advance, deployed as skirmishers.[5] Two companies of the Fourth Massachusetts, three companies of the One Hundred Tenth New York, and one company of the Thirty-eighth Massachusetts followed the skirmish line, armed with hand grenades and rifles. Colonel Oliver P. Gooding's Third Brigade advanced immediately behind the grenadiers, with the Thirty-first Massachusetts, under Lieutenant Colonel W. S. B. Hopkins, leading the brigade and carrying cotton bags with which to fill the ditch in front of the parapet.[6] The Thirty-eighth Massachusetts, commanded by Major James P. Richardson, and the Fifty-third Massachusetts, by Colonel John W. Kimball, followed the Thirty-first; and the One Hundred Fifty-sixth New York, under Major John Gray, brought up the rear of the brigade. Colonel Hawkes Fearing, with part of the Second Brigade, consisting of the One Hundred Thirty-third New York, under Colonel Leonard D. H. Currie,[7] and the One Hundred Seventy-third New York, under Captain George W. Rogers, followed in the rear of Colonel Gooding. The rear of General Paine's assault column consisted of Colonel Samuel Ferris' First Brigade, composed of the Twenty-eighth Connecticut, five companies of the Fourth Massachusetts, and five companies of the One Hundred Tenth New York. Captain Ormand F. Nims and his field battery followed, along with a small detachment of pioneers.

The battlefield was quiet as the Third Division advanced to within ninety yards of the left (Union) face of the Priest Cap. Paine walked to the front of the skirmish line and yelled out the order to attack. The men surged forward, but had moved only a few feet when the First Mississippi and the Forty-ninth Alabama gave them a terrific volley.[8] Scores of Yankees fell dead or wounded, among them General Paine, whose leg was broken below the knee by a rifle ball.[9]

The Union forces drove onward with relentless fury, endangering the Forty-ninth Alabama's position. Portions of the First Mississippi, which was actually holding the Priest Cap, were pulled down to reinforce the hard-pressed Alabamans, leaving a gap in the Confederate line.[10] The Thirty-first Massachusetts Infantry succeeded in partly filling the ditch with cotton bags, and troops from the Fourth Wisconsin, Eighth New Hampshire, Thirty-eighth Massachusetts, and the Fifty-third Massachusetts crossed the ditch, climbed over the parapet, and entered the Confederate stronghold at the exposed gap.[11] Port Hudson's defenses were now breached, but the rest of the Third Division could not or would not advance.

With General Paine out of action, his regiments fell into disorder and became thoroughly mixed up.[12] Colonel Henry W. Birge was dispatched by Grover to take command of Paine's division, but before he arrived the impetus of the first great assault had been spent. It was a critical moment of the battle as the men of the First Mississippi moved back to hurl themselves on the Yankees who had entered their defenses. A short but desperate fight ensued, in which the Mississippians suffered heavy casualties. The Yankees inside the Port Hudson defenses were bayoneted, shot, clubbed, or captured, and the threat to the Priest Cap was at least temporarily lessened.[13]

Reforming, the Yankees made repeated assaults against the Confederate works. In several instances their grenadiers reached the shelter of the ditch and flung their grenades over the parapets. But the Alabamans and Mississippians caught the missiles before they could explode and flung them back into the faces of the enemy.[14] After throwing their missiles, the grenadiers unslung their rifles and joined in with the skirmishers—at least those who survived having their grenades thrown back at them. The cotton-bag bearers also joined in with the skirmishers, raking the Confederates with heavy blasts of rifle fire.

Paine's skirmish line and the Third Brigade were badly scattered along the left (Union) face of the Priest Cap. Colonel Birge sent the Second and First Brigades in to attack. The Second Brigade apparently hit the Priest Cap. Colonel Currie was wounded while mounting the breastworks, and his men were driven back. The First Brigade, under Colonel Ferris, hit to the right of the Priest Cap, but the attack was not vigorously pressed. Some confusion resulted as Colonel Ferris' brigade became entangled with Weitzel's left.[15] The brunt of the fighting fell on the First Mississippi, causing the members of the regiment to run short of ammunition—percussion caps, especially. Beall's artillery was able to give the infantry but little support, as most of his guns were silenced as soon as they opened fire.[16] By 8 A.M. the battle was over. The ground in front of the right (Confederate) of the Priest Cap was blue—colored by the uniforms of the fallen Federals. At one point in the ditch fourteen dead Yankees were sprawled on top of each other.[17] Paine's Third Division had utterly failed in its attack; however, Grover was not yet through.

Weitzel's division had been ordered to attack simultaneously with that of Paine's, but various complications prevented Weitzel from commencing his forward movement before about 7 A.M. The movement of the troops in the pre-dawn darkness caused some of the Federals to become lost. Weitzel's battle plan called for Lieutenant Colonel Willoughby Babcock to lead a skirmishing party of two regiments against the right (Union) face of the Priest Cap. The Twelfth Connecticut, under Lieutenant Colonel Frank Peck, was to enter the covered way and upon coming out form a skirmish line to the left. The Seventy-fifth New York, under Captain William H. Cray, was to flank right and form a skirmish line to pin down the Arkansans and Mississippians. With the Confederates held down by the skirmishers' fire, Jacob Van Zandt's Ninety-first New York was to advance to the edge of the ditch and rake the inside of the parapet with hand grenades.[18] Colonel Samuel Mansfield's Twenty-fourth Connecticut Regiment was to advance behind the skirmishers and fill the ditch with bags of cotton. The storming column was to move up behind the Twenty-fourth Connecticut, cross the filled-in ditch, climb the parapet, and capture Port Hudson. The storming column consisted of four brigades. The lead brigade was Weitzel's old unit, commanded by Colonel Elisha B. Smith, consisting of the Eighth Vermont and the One Hundred Fourteenth and One Hundred Sixteenth New York. The First, Second, and Third Brigades, Fourth Division, headed respectively by Colonels Joseph Morgan, William K. Kimball, and Henry Birge, the total numbering fourteen regiments, were to follow Smith in.

Weitzel's men were not enthusiastic about attacking on a Sunday morning, and there were those among them who anticipated bad luck because of the sacrilege.[19] As the Federal troops advanced into the covered way, trouble began. The Twelfth Connecticut was not in position, having been guided in the wrong direction by an incompetent staff officer.[20] Lieutenant Colonel Babcock ordered the Seventy-fifth New York to move on out without bothering to wait for the Twelfth Connecticut.[21]

Despite numerous precautions to muffle the sounds of troops moving, such as padding the roads and bridges with cotton, the Confederates heard the advancing New Yorkers in the covered way and opened fire on them. The New Yorkers reached the end of the sunken road, which ran within eighty yards of the Confederate works, and charged forward.[22] They advanced only a short distance before being driven to cover by the hot Confederate fire. The tardy Twelfth Connecticut entered the sunken road and moved forward to support the New Yorkers; but before they reached the end of the road, they ran into the wounded who were being brought back through. A wild traffic jam ensued as the wounded New Yorkers yelled for the Connecticut men to get out of the sunken road and help the Seventy-fifth, which was in serious trouble. Finally, coming out of the road the men of the Twelfth launched an enthusiastic but haphazard attack against the Confederates. Like the Seventy-fifth New York, the Twelfth was soon driven to cover, where the men began sniping at the Southerners.[23] In the desperate fighting in front of the ditch, Lieutenant Colonel Babcock was wounded, leaving his skirmishers without a leader; however, positions were gained within twenty to fifty yards of the Confederate works.

The Ninety-first New York moved forward to launch its grenade attack.[24] Reaching the ditch, the Yankee grenadiers hurled their five-pound percussion grenades at the Southerners. A few of their missiles burst along the top of the parapet, spattering the Southerners with dirt, but most of them landed inside the parapet. The canny Confederates had covered the ground with blankets, and the grenades landed on them harmlessly. Having thrown their grenades, the Yankee soldiers unslung their rifles and started crossing the ditch. To their amazement the New Yorkers saw their own grenades being thrown back at them from the top of the parapet. Despite the slaughter caused by the exploding grenades, the surviving New Yorkers launched a furious assault against the breastworks. With reckless courage the Ninety-first's color-bearer, Private Samuel Townsend, Company K, attempted to plant the "Stars and Stripes" on top of the parapet. Of Southern origin, but loyal to the Union, Townsend was recognized by the Alabaman who shot him down—his own brother.[25]

The men of the Ninety-first New York fared no better than

their comrades of the Twelfth Connecticut and the Seventy-fifth New York. The ground was littered with bodies of dead Yanks, and yet the main assault had not begun. Finally Smith's brigade came into action. Making their way through the crowded sunken road, amid shouts of confusion and disorder, the men of the One Hundred Fourteenth New York emerged from the road and delivered a gallant attack on the Confederates which was repulsed with heavy loss.[26] The New Yorkers reached the ditch and then halted. Badly shot up, they retreated, leaving their colors lying in front of the ditch.[27] The Twenty-fourth Connecticut had failed to fill in the ditch, and the thirty-pound bags of cotton were scattered over the ground—some with their carriers crouched behind them, firing at the Southerners. The rest of Weitzel's brigade moved forward against the breastworks, using the ravines and gullies as cover. Colonel Smith was shot down minutes later. "You must not stop on my account; your duty is to be in the advance," Smith told some of his men who tried to help him off the field.[28] Lieutenant Colonel John B. Van Petten assumed command of the brigade, leading it forward in a desperate attempt to shatter the Confederate line.

From the Confederate works there came an almost continual pattern of red flashes.[29] "Like leaves before an autumn blast," Northerners were falling on all sides.[30] In the face of the terrible fire the Union men halted and then fell back, taking cover where they could behind tree stumps, cotton bales, or on the face of the parapet. It was a scene of indescribable chaos. The regiments had lost all traces of cohesion, and it was every man for himself. In the rear a report was circulating that the Federals had effected a lodgment inside Port Hudson. When queried as to the validity of the report, General Weitzel replied, "No, we've not got a foothold inside." Captain Homer Sprague immediately asked, "Why can't we go in at once?" Weitzel answered, "We can go in if the officers and men will only do their duty." Sprague then asked, "Have the enemy massed their troops at this point?" Weitzel replied, "I don't think they have, and if they have, we've got more men right here between us and the works than their whole garrison." The conversation abruptly ended as an order from Banks arrived directing Weitzel to storm Port Hudson no matter what the cost.[31] Weitzel immediately ordered Colonel Holcomb to take in the First Brigade, which began a steady advance toward the Confederate works. Colonel Simon G. Jerrard, Twenty-second Maine, waved his sword in the air and shouted, "Come on my brave boys; follow me!" [32] The Yankees dashed forward, running into a hot fire which confused them.

The Third Brigade was ordered forward to support Holcomb, the first of the troops arriving just as Holcomb was rallying his men for the big attack. "All I ask of you is to follow me!" Holcomb shouted. "Will you follow me?" Fifty men shouted, "Yes." [33] The rest sat quietly on the ground, declining to answer the question. Troops from the Third Brigade proved more amenable to the idea of an attack, and Holcomb gave the order, "Forward." The troops of both the First and Third Brigades surged forward. Holcomb fell, his brains spattered on the ground, and his troops, confused and disorganized by the difficult terrain over which they were passing, began to falter and finally to give ground. Several hundred men took shelter in a ravine only a few yards short of the Confederate works. The Twenty-sixth Maine Infantry Regiment, Third Brigade, reached a point within twenty feet of the works.

Under cover of the sheltering ravine, from five hundred to a thousand men collected before ten o'clock. The Union "brass" began to congregate at a point only thirty yards from the Confederate lines, discussing the situation and trying to decide on a course of action. Colonel N. H. Hubbard said he was willing to follow if someone else would start the attack. Major C. A. Burt said he would do likewise, but he did not believe the Rebel works could be held even if seized. Colonel Simon G. Jerrard expressed himself most forcibly, saying, "If General Banks wants to go in there, let him go in and be damned. I won't slaughter my men that way." [34] Lieutenant Nicholas Day succinctly remarked, "I started out this morning with the determination to be a hell of a man! I've been a hell of a fellow long enough. If anybody else wants to be a hell of a fellow, I've no objections! But it's too damned risky!" [35]

For the moment the assault was not renewed, but Banks sent orders that a storming party of two hundred men should be organized to lead the attack. He promised promotions to everyone who volunteered. The volunteers were soon collected, but the regimental commanders held a council of war, unanimously agreeing that the storming party was a "fool" idea. Fortunately, Banks decided to countermand the order.

To distract attention from the attacks of Generals Paine and Weitzel, Augur launched a sham attack about 3:45 A.M. on the Confederate works northeast of the Citadel. Augur's men expended great quantities of rifle ammunition in order to draw Confederate attention from the actual attacks.

Many of the Union soldiers went into battle with canteens filled with whisky.[36] After several hours of sharpshooting, a Union infantry regiment advanced to support the Forty-ninth Massachusetts, which was on the firing line. Between drinks of whisky, the men in the support regiment blazed away with their rifles in the general direction of the Confederate works. As their bullets began to spatter the Forty-ninth Massachusetts, the Yanks shouted, "Fire higher!" The shout was carried along the battle front, and "the miserable fellows thought, in their drunken valor that they were the nearest regiment to the foe, or caring little and seeing no chance to hit rebels, concluded to do some kind of execution. . . . So imminent was the danger from their guns that it became a questionable matter which was the safer side of the logs." [37]

Augur's skirmishers made a lot of noise but accomplished no military gain. The Sixteenth Arkansas returned the fire with enthusiasm, exchanging volley for volley. The Arkansans' loss was slight, one man being killed—Lieutenant Colonel Benjamin F. Pixlee, a hero of Corinth. Lieutenant A. M. Trawich, on the firing line for more than an hour, and worn out from exertion, was offered relief by Pixlee, who said, "Lieutenant Trawich, you are tired, let me get in there and shoot a few Yankees. My carbine is much longer-ranged than your musket." Trawich replied, "No, Colonel; this is too dangerous for you. Many balls have passed close by me." Pixlee insisted. Trawich then sat down and began reading from a small Testament while Pixlee shot at Yanks. Several minutes later the lieutenant heard a thudding sound and turned to see Pixlee falling—shot through the head.[38]

While Paine was having his difficulties with the Confederate left, General Dwight endeavored to break into Port Hudson along the extreme Confederate right. The original plan of operation as agreed upon the night before was for Dwight to batter his way in at the Citadel while Augur distracted the Southerners with his feigned attack. Around 4 A.M. Dwight ordered the Sixth Michigan, under Colonel Edward Bacon, and the Fourteenth Maine, under Colonel Thomas W. Porter, to force their way past the Citadel along the river front.[39] Upon passing under the bluffs, the two regiments were to attack the Confederate works from the rear. Captain Henry Stark of the Sixth Michigan led the way with a detachment of fifty men, his orders being to occupy and hold General Gardner's headquarters.[40] Captain John Cordon followed Stark with two hundred men. His orders were to seize the Citadel and fire a rocket as a signal for Bacon and Porter to advance. The Yanks were to climb up steps which supposedly ran up the side of the Citadel, facing the river. Stark was ordered to capture the first Confederate soldier he found and use him as a guide to Gardner's headquarters. According to Lieutenant William Trash, Grierson had orders to charge through the Citadel's sally-port, saber the Confederate gunners, and ride to the center of Port Hudson, where Dwight was to join him to celebrate the victory.[41] Captains Stark and Cordon found their orders impossible to execute, and Grierson simply ignored his. Thus, the movement came to naught as the regiments under Bacon and Porter could not advance.

The Sixth Michigan and the One Hundred Twenty-eighth New York, commanded by Colonel James Smith, were finally sent forward against the Citadel as skirmishers. Soon after sunrise Dwight sent Lieutenant Colonel Henry W. Blair's Fifteenth New Hampshire and Colonel Joseph Sheldon's Twenty-sixth Connecticut forward along the Mount Pleasant Road. The two regiments were thrown forward in line of battle under heavy fire, and advanced to within about three hundred yards of the Citadel, where the Mount Pleasant Road was intersected by a deep gully.[42]

Under heavy fire from two of Captain R. M. Boone's 12-pounders, and from Lieutenant M. E. Pratt's "The Virginia," a 24-pounder, the Union troops were forced to take shelter in the gully. Some worked their way forward to support the Sixth Michigan and the One Hundred Twenty-eighth New York, which were already engaged with the Confederates. The attack had degenerated into a sharpshooting spree, with the men of Miles' Legion trading shots with the four Union regiments for the rest of the day. The Federals who were pinned down in the gully suffered terribly from heat, hunger, and thirst, being unable to withdraw before nightfall.[43]

General F. S. Nickerson's brigade moved to support the attack on Miles' Legion, but failed to become seriously involved in the fighting.[44] The only thing gained by Dwight's movements was the hill in front of the Citadel, which was permanently occupied. Although it was only 11 A.M., the battlefield was virtually silent. The serious fighting was over, but the suffering was only beginning, for more than a thousand wounded Yankee soldiers lay sprawled on the battlefield, plagued by thirst and tormented by flies. The gallant General Paine still lay within easy rifle shot of the Confederate works; his only hope of protection from the blistering sun was that he lay between two rows of cotton. The general dared not even cover his face with his cap lest the movement draw a shot.[45] Several Yankee soldiers attempted to crawl to Paine's aid. Private J. B. Woods, Company E, Thirty-first Massachusetts, was shot dead less than five feet from his mark. Other Yanks followed Woods; they all fell with bullets in their bodies.[46] Private Patrick Cohen of the One Hundred Thirty-first New York managed to throw Paine a canteen of water, which probably saved his life.[47] Charles Constatine of the Twelfth Connecticut "took off his equipment, crawled to him, took him on his back, and carried him safely to a place where he could be reached by the stretcher bearers." [48] Colonel Michael Kirk Bryan of the One Hundred Seventy-fifth New York, part of

Augur's command, was not so fortunate. With both legs broken by bullets, Bryan lay in the sun for two hours before expiring.[49]

At Port Hudson the Yankees had converted nearby plantation buildings into field hospitals for the wounded.[50] Surgery was performed in the buildings, and the wounded were given the best treatment obtainable. Piles of arms and legs decorated the grounds outside the operating rooms. The wounded were then transported to Springfield Landing, and from there to Baton Rouge. Steamers such as the *Iberville* carried the wounded Yanks to Baton Rouge, where they were moved to the permanent hospital in the old arsenal buildings. The hospitals were fitted out with everything that the sanitary and Christian commissions could think of to alleviate the sufferings of the wounded.[51]

The staggering figure of 1,805 Federal soldiers dead, wounded, or prisoners bore mute testimony to the ferocity of the battle. When asked why he had ordered the May 27 assault, Banks replied, "The people of the North demand blood, sir." [52] After the June 14 assault, enough blood had been shed to surfeit even the most blood-thirsty Abolitionist. Four thousand men had already fallen, and the Confederates were still determined to fight on.

X

Grim Days

ON Monday, June 15, 1863, there was quiet after the strenuous exertions of the previous day's battle and the twenty-three days of constant fighting since the investment began. General Banks issued an order of congratulations to his troops that seemed to overlook the previous day's repulse. The commanding officer expressed confidence in an immediate victory. "One more advance and they are ours!"[1] The troops were called upon to volunteer to form a storming column of a thousand men. An officer of the Twelfth Connecticut said, "Once more the men were marched to corps headquarters, formed in a hollow square, and treated to an encouraging speech from General Banks."[2] Intent upon another assault, Banks offered various glories and rewards to the men who volunteered. A colonel who happened to admire the discourse said it was fit "to be pronounced in the United States Senate." Another colonel, lacking enthusiasm for Banks's military ability, commented it was "just fit." Upon the conclusion of the oratory, the Twelfth Connecticut's brigade commander shouted, "Three cheers for General Banks!" The officers shouted, "Hurrah!" and the men looked on in sullen silence.[3]

As an inducement for volunteering for the storming party, Banks promised that all volunteers would receive medals and promotions. Notwithstanding his generosity, there was no immediate rush to join the "forlorn hope." After the slaughter of May 27 and June 14, the Union troops had suffered much loss of confidence in Banks's ability.[4] The men of the One Hundred Twenty-eighth New York were unhappy with the forlorn hope

94

idea; their theory was that the whole army should attack at the same time without an artillery barrage to alert the Confederates.[5]

Most of the volunteers came from units which had suffered but light losses in the fighting. The Eighth New Hampshire, which had fought stoutly, contributed only three men to the forlorn hope; the Thirty-eighth Massachusetts gave only one. The Forty-ninth Massachusetts refused to contribute a single man, whereupon Banks ordered seventeen of the men to "volunteer" or else.[6] The Twelfth Connecticut contributed thirty-two volunteers, who according to Captain William DeForest, "were a curious medley as to character, some of them being our best and bravest men, while others were mere rapscallions, whose sole object was, probably, to get the whiskey ration issued to the forlorn hope." [7]

Colonel Henry W. Birge of the Thirteenth Connecticut volunteered to lead the stormers, and 241 of his men agreed to follow him. The volunteers were collected at a camp about a mile to the rear of the Union line. The men "were carefully drilled, instructed, and held in readiness to move at five minutes' notice." [8] Scaling ladders were constructed, and the troops trained in their use. Birge organized his men into two battalions of five companies each. Lieutenant Colonel Van Petten was given command of the first battalion, and Lieutenant Colonel A. S. Bickmore received command of the second. The total number of men in the unit was 1,036.

While Banks was indulging in oratory and the volunteers were being collected, hundreds of dead and wounded Union soldiers still lay untended on the battlefield. Still other wounded were being cared for by Gardner's men within the Port. During the evening of June 15 Banks sent a flag of truce to the Confederate commander, asking Gardner to receive drugs and other items for the wounded prisoners in Confederate hands.[9] Gardner promptly consented to receive all such items, assuring the Federal commander that they would be used as purposed. At this same time Gardner expressed his surprise that no cessation of fighting had been requested by Banks to remove the Federal dead and wounded, who now had lain upon an open field under a blazing sun for two days. The drugs were sent in, but nothing was said about removing the dead and wounded.[10]

A party of Confederates went out to aid the wounded Federals, whose pitiful cries kept ringing in their ears. But the Southerners were fired on and were forced to return to their works, leaving the remaining wounded abandoned on the hot field. "A Confederate, more tender-hearted than Banks, was shot by the enemy while carrying a canteen of water to a wounded Federal who lay near the works." [11]

After failing to drive the Confederates out of Port Hudson by brute force, the Yankees apparently decided to try to stench them out. The Southerners offered to carry the dead and wounded Yanks over to the Union lines, but the offer was refused. When one of Dwight's officers begged him to use his influence to see that the Confederate offer was accepted, he indignantly gave the following reply:

No, sir, it's all a stratagem of the enemy to get the dead carcasses carried away from before their works. They know that they will be stunk out if the bodies rot there, and they cannot get them away on account of our fire. No, sir, I'll stink the rebels out of the citadel with the dead bodies of these damned volunteers if I cannot make the cowards take it by storm, as I have ordered them to do.[12]

The odor from the decomposing bodies having become almost unbearable by June 17, Gardner sent a message under a flag of truce to Banks, asking him to please bury his dead. Banks replied that he had no dead on the battlefield. Gardner then requested Beall to send a flag of truce to Augur, asking him to bury the dead lying in front of the First Mississippi and the Forty-ninth Alabama. Augur agreed to a flag of truce and generously allowed the Southerners to drag the Union dead—some 260—over to the Union lines, where his men took over the grisly task of burying the decomposing bodies.[13] The Union dead in front of Fort Desperate and the adjoining works were not buried, and their bodies could be seen from the breastworks up to the time of the surrender.

On the evening of June 16 the Federals made a weak attack

against the extreme Confederate left (Colonel Shelby's command) which was easily repulsed.[14] After this movement, affairs at Port Hudson settled down to a routine of sharpshooting, bombardment, and trench raids. Despite the sharpshooting and shelling, there was apparently little bad feeling between the Union and Confederate troops on the firing line. From June 16 onward for nearly a week an informal truce existed between the "Johnny Rebs" and "Billy Yanks." However, the truce extended only to the white troops.[15] During this strange interlude a curious *entente cordiale* existed between the soldiers of both armies. White handkerchiefs would wave above the trenches, and within seconds the blue and the gray would be out in the open, yelling insults at one another. No man violated the informal truce, for his buddies would have dealt harshly with him. After awhile someone would yell, "Look out now Yanks; we are going to fire." The men would scamper back to their trenches, and the firing would soon recommence.[16]

In still another instance, Sergeant Lewis Child and three other members of the Eighth Vermont Infantry climbed over the Confederate works and engaged the Southerners in conversation until a graycoat officer came along and told them "to get out or be shot." [17] During an informal armistice the Confederates thoughtfully provided the Yanks with copies of the Port Hudson newspaper which refuted Union claims that the Confederates had refused to permit them to carry their wounded off the battlefield on June 14.[18]

In between the unofficial truces, things were pretty grim.[19] The sharpshooters on both sides often grew reckless. Private Samuel O. Horn, Company B, Eighth Vermont, returned from the rear to the firing line on the morning of June 20 clad in a clean white shirt. Horn casually exposed his head and shoulders over the top of the trench. A Confederate sharpshooter spotted the white shirt and blazed away at it. The slug missed and Horn shouted, "You are no sort of a shot! You couldn't hit the broadside of a barn. Try again." Reloading, the Confederate did try again, hitting Horn between the eyes and killing him.[20]

Various tricks were resorted to by sharpshooters to draw

enemy fire, thus providing good targets. Frequently a man would put his cap on the tip of his ramrod and raise it over the edge of the parapet where the enemy could see it. It was sure to be immediately riddled by several rifle balls. On one occasion a "daredevil Johnny Reb raised his hat, which had his head in it, and took a good look at the other side." Instantly there came a shout from the Yankee lines: "If you put your head in that hat we'll take a shot at it." [21]

Sharpshooting was not the only hazard for the men in the trenches. Disease struck the soldiers of both armies. Constant exposure to the elements and the lack of proper facilities put hundreds of Confederates and Yankees in the hospitals and cemeteries. Scurvy, the filthy condition of the drinking water, and the nervous strain of trench warfare depleted the blue ranks,[22] and malaria was a big crippler among the Confederates. The Confederates' stock of medicines was even shorter than their supply of provisions. Quinine and ipecac were used in the first few weeks, but the supply was soon exhausted. Many of the sick preferred to remain on the firing line, where they could at least get in a few more licks at the "Bluebellies."

When the siege began, the Confederates had but ten days' rations of meat and bread on hand, although there was a good supply of molasses, sugar, and salt.[23] By mid-June the supply of bread was completely gone and the Confederates were using ground corn as a substitute. Union artillery wrecked their grist mill, which was located behind Commissary Hill, destroying several thousand bushels of grain. The Confederates had a small portable mill at Port Hudson but no power to operate it. In order to work the mill they were forced to resort to ingenuity— using the old locomotive of the Clinton and Port Hudson Railroad as a source of power. They placed the locomotive on blocks, passed the belt of the corn-mill around one of the wheels, and started the engine, and in this fashion were able "to furnish meal at the rate of several miles an hour." [24] The new mill was at the railroad depot, under the command of Captain B. Jones. Lying in their trenches at night, the Yanks could hear the locomotive engine working. Realizing the importance of the mill, "whose location the batteries are crazy to know, that they may seal its doom," the Federals made repeated attempts to locate it, yet were never successful until the last day of bloodshed.[25] A private of the One Hundred Sixty-fifth New York, captured on May 27, escaped from Port Hudson and revealed the location of the mill. Banks ordered Captain Nims to take his guns, cross the river, and shell the mill. Guided by the escaped soldier, Lieutenant Hall and the first section of the battery set up their guns on the levee directly opposite the Port Hudson depot. The Yanks opened fire on the mill, but their aim was high. The Confederates answered with a blast from a 42-pounder which tore the private into a bloody pulp. Horrified by the accuracy of the Confederates' fire, the Yanks withdrew, leaving the mill to grind out the last corn meal without interference.[26] Without it the Southerners would have been forced to surrender from hunger weeks earlier.

In addition to razing the old grist mill, Union artillery pounded the whole of Port Hudson with an unrelenting rain of destruction. Exploding shells shattered the windows of the Port Hudson church, and glass fragments became mixed in with the field peas stored there by the Confederate commissary. It was no unusual sight to see hungry Confederates spitting out pieces of glass between bites of corn bread.[27]

By the end of June, the food supply being almost exhausted, mules and horses were slaughtered by the Confederates. Up to this time eating horse meat or mule flesh had not been thought of, although dozens of animals had been killed by shells in all parts of the garrison. But when the last cow—a very poor one—was handed out, an order to issue horse and mule meat was given. "Many of the soldiers swore they wouldn't eat it; while others, just as determined, said they would eat anything 'Daddy Long Legs,' as they humorously called Gen. Gardner, would issue to them as rations. But the beginning was everything—who was to take the initiatory in the matter, so as to give the example to others, there was the rub. Gen. Gardner . . . ordered fifteen pounds from the first mule killed, for his own mess, to show his men that he was willing to eat of the same dainties provided for them. His example was followed by nearly all the command." [28]

"No soldier will ever forget his first horse meat breakfast," Linn Tanner, a Port Hudson veteran, wrote after the surrender.[29] It was a comical sight to watch facial expressions as the men viewed dishes of "hot [horse] steak, fried in its own grease," or the big "chunks" of boiled mule as they floated on the top in a bucket of stew. One after the other tackled the task of eating it. Now and then a "Ye-h, ye-h, ye haw!" was heard in imitation of a jackass or mule, or occasionally someone mocked a trotting horse. Done in pure jollity, these imitations became contagious and added toward lifting Confederate morale.

Many Southern boys soon forgot their first unedible-looking piece of coarse horse flesh. Linn Tanner discovered it was not hard to persuade himself "that a piece of fat mule was not so bad." As he attempted to eat his rations in the secluded area of a ravine, he saw a buddy, known affectionately as "Growling Grif," who was looking upset. "What's the matter, Grif?" he asked. With an oath, Grif replied, "That d—— commissary sergeant had my mule killed this morning." The conversation continued, and after awhile Grif added, "Well, I don't suppose you care about it; but I do. Old Jack had a sore back and I wanted to cure it up." Tanner threw his meat away, but later retrieved it.[30]

Private Edward McMorries declared that mule "had a flavor somewhat like turkey, but it tasted like nothing else . . . except mule." McMorries also tried corn bread "shortened with mule grease," but his stomach rebelled against that.[31] In their desperate need for food, the Confederates tried other "delicacies" besides horse and mule, even resorting to the rats that infested the trenches and shattered houses. At Confederate headquarters General Gardner and his staff dined on "broiled rats, sugar and weavily peas" during the last few days of the siege.[32] Toward the last, even the soldiers' pet dogs went into the stew pot, providing some of the men with a hot meal.[33]

The Confederates were hungry, and Banks knew this; however, he felt that to starve Port Hudson into submission might take too long a time. Thus, he prepared to make a third assault. In order to give the storming party maximum protection, he ordered that construction on the old siege approaches be resumed and that new works be begun. At least temporarily, the shovel would supersede the bayonet.

On June 17 Major David C. Houston, who had hitherto been directing siege operations, broke down under the strain and was replaced by Captain John C. Palfrey. The new chief engineer decided that the key point to the Confederate defenses was the Priest Cap. Palfrey's plan was to extend an old siege approach to the left of that position, to erect trench cavaliers (sharpshooting platforms) to enfilade the interior of the Confederate works, and to run a zigzag approach into its ditch. At the same time, another siege approach would be started against Fort Desperate. Once the two approaches were completed, the Confederate lines could be shattered and the two positions carried by assault.

On June 14, after the capture of the bluff opposite the Citadel, Dwight directed Joe Bailey to erect a powerful battery which could enfilade the Confederate right and silence the Citadel. By June 20 "the bluff was surmounted by a row of redoubts, occupied by seventeen pieces of heavy ordnance. Some of these were pivot guns and could be used both for front and rear." [34] Dwight's new gun position, officially Battery No. 24, contained a tremendous concentration of fire power—two 20-pound Parrotts, three 24-pound rifles, two 9-inch Dahlgrens, one 8-inch howitzer, two Napoleons, and two 10-inch mortars—and was located less than two hundred yards from Confederate Battery No. XI.[35]

The Confederates were not greatly alarmed by Dwight's battery. In fact, Gardner was reported to have been so pleased over the Federals pulling down guns from points where they were hurting Port Hudson to this new position that he ordered his men not to fire on Bailey's work parties, lest it hamper them. According to Lieutenant Colonel Edward Bacon, some of the "rebel officers even offered to come over and help" construct the battery.[36]

In order to provide a safe command post for Dwight, Bailey built a large bombproof near Battery No. 24. The command post had "the appearance of a large, well packed mound, in the shape of half a globe." [37] There were three observation slots in the side facing the Citadel, through which Dwight could safely observe the progress of the siege. The reverse side was left open in order to provide light and ventilation. The post was provided with a floor, table, chairs, and several cabinets of good food and liquor.

Battery No. 24 commenced shelling the Citadel on June 20, but the bombardment did so little damage that Bailey obtained permission from Dwight to begin a series of zigzags against Confederate Battery No. XI. To divert attention from the main approach, Bailey began work on still another series of zigzags leading toward the southeastern angle of the Confederate defense line, but starting from a ravine well to the right of the seventeen-gun battery.[38] A zigzag approach was started by Colonel E. D. Johnson's Twenty-first Maine Infantry, running from the ravine near the Slaughter house to a position less than four hundred yards from the Confederate works. Lieutenant J. B. Rawles's and Lieutenant J. M. Bains's batteries were put in position at the end of this approach. A fifth siege approach was begun— against Fort Desperate.[39]

Moving the zigzag forward in the hot Louisiana sun was killing work for the Union white troops; consequently, thousands of slaves were taken from neighboring plantations to provide a stable labor supply for digging. Brutally treated by their "liberators," the Negroes rapidly advanced the parallels toward the Confederate lines.[40] While these zigzags were being advanced, numerous trench raids and skirmishes occurred, interrupting the work. On June 20, at about 3 A.M., Lieutenant Bankston of Miles' Legion and fifty men sallied out from the Port Hudson defenses and drove in the Federals' skirmish line.[41] On June 22 the men of the Twenty-eighth Maine Infantry made a sortie against Beall's center. They were repulsed with a loss of three killed, nine wounded, and twenty-six missing.[42] Before dawn on June 23 two Union regiments attempted to take the Plains Store road sally port in a surprise attack, but the Arkansans discovered them and drove them back with loss.[43]

Despite these and other engagements, the Federals drove their parallels ever closer to Port Hudson. The ground was eminently suited for siege work, but "there probably were not ten men in the army who had ever seen a sap, and half of them were generals." [44] The directions of the saps (trenches used to approach an enemy's works) were laid out by the draftsmen and civil assistants of the engineer department. The fascines were tied with twine, and barrels and cracker boxes were used for gabions. A sugar hogshead full of cotton was used for a sap roller, and bales of cotton were buried in the embankments to provide better cover for the men.[45] At first, cotton bales were used to protect the heads of the saps, but this experiment did not prove too successful because the Confederates shot flaming arrows into the cotton, or sallied out and lit it with firebrands.[46]

On June 25 Corporal L. H. Skelton, Company F, First Mississippi, crawled from the Priest Cap in broad daylight and under heavy fire to the head of the enemy's sap and set the cotton bales afire. Skelton returned to the Priest Cap unhurt. As the Yankees extinguished the flames, he volunteered for a second try and, making his way back to the head of the sap, relit the bales, holding the Federals off until the fire was well started. Equipped with two captured Enfield rifles, Skelton crawled back to the Priest Cap still unwounded. Impressed by the incident, General Gardner issued General Order No. 57, praising him for his courage and determination.[47]

To protect the head of their sap running toward the Priest Cap, the Federals erected a great trench cavalier of sugar hogsheads filled with dirt and covered with sandbags. From this towering platform Union sharpshooters could pick off any Southerner who attempted to burn the cotton bales. As an added protection, the Yanks covered the cotton bales with dirt. With the advance of the parallels, cannon were dragged forward through the trenches, and batteries were established just a few yards from the Confederate works. The Union gunners opened fire from their new position, and the Confederates retaliated by picking off Union gun commanders as they sighted their pieces—an occurrence not conducive to careful aiming on the part of their successors. To protect their gunners, the Yanks covered each gun embrasure with "a plate of iron, in which was a hole of the size of a muzzle of a gun, temporarily covered with a sandbag." [48]

The hole was only left uncovered for a few seconds as the men aimed their weapons. The sandbag was then replaced.

The sap against Fort Desperate was run forward in a straight line, marred only by slight zigzags, to give the working party some protection from the fire of Colonel Ben Johnson's Fifteenth Arkansas Regiment. The directness of the approach necessitated the use of a sap roller. Colonel Johnson's men constructed galleries under the parapet and leading up to the ditch, enabling them to sharpshoot the Federals. A cavalier was constructed on top of the parapet of Fort Desperate, allowing the Arkansans to shoot down into the advancing sap.[49] Grover's men drove their sap to within ninety feet of Fort Desperate before the fire from the sharpshooting tower forced them to abandon their digging on or about July 3. If Grover's men had been able to advance the sap closer, Colonel Johnson planned to storm the head of the sap and fight it out.

To meet the threat against his left, Gardner concentrated twelve of his remaining usable field guns and almost half his effective infantrymen.[50] The sap against Fort Desperate having finally failed, the Confederate left was in a perfect position to support Beall, commanding the center, in case of an attack on the Priest Cap.

The siege approach against the Priest Cap started in a north-westerly direction from Duryea's Battery No. 12. The first parallel was nearly three hundred yards in length, and it gradually curved to the west against Foster's Creek and then ran southward, curving into the second parallel, which ran from the left angle of the Priest Cap to a point about two hundred yards from the Clinton–Port Hudson road. The second parallel was nearly a quarter mile in length and varied from about twenty to fifty feet near the Priest Cap and the line to the right held by the Forty-ninth Alabama.[51] On July 1 Colonel Willoughby Babcock wrote in his diary: "Our men now have covered approaches to within 20 or 30 feet of the enemy's works, our batteries are being constantly planted on smaller concentric circles and everything looks well." [52] Grover's men constructed a second cavalier a short distance from the first—both being about ninety feet from the right angle (Confederate) of the Priest Cap.

The third major sap, running against the Citadel, was probably the easiest to construct. The Yanks started the sap on the bank of the Mississippi River to the left of Mount Pleasant and ran it forward in five stretches of fifty to sixty yards each, onto the slope of the hill on which the Citadel was located. The head of the sap was less than a dozen yards from the Citadel, and the Federals decided to try mining the Confederate position. At about the same time, Grover's engineers started two mines against the Priest Cap. Once the tunnels were complete the Federals planned to explode the mines—heavy charges of explosives—underneath the two Confederate positions. The galleries required no framing, and the Yanks could drive them sixty to seventy feet underground without artificial ventilation.[53]

Realizing their danger, the Confederate engineers at the Priest Cap began digging a countermine. Lieutenant Fred Y. Dabney supervised the work—the men digging with hand trowels. When the gallery was finally completed, an explosive charge was put in place. Dabney attached a friction primer to the charge and a length of piano wire to the friction primer. The gallery was cleared of men and, from inside the Priest Cap, Dabney pulled the wire.[54] Shortly after midnight on July 3 the Yanks, working in the Union gallery, were amazed as the tunnel collapsed on them. Great quantities of dirt were thrown in all directions, and several picks and shovels flew through the air, landing inside the Confederate lines. The Yanks dug themselves out and counted heads. Miraculously, no one was seriously hurt, but the Federals shifted their efforts to the other mine running under the Priest Cap.[55]

The Confederate troops did not spend all their time digging holes in the ground. On June 26 Lieutenant A. S. McKennon and thirty volunteers from the Sixteenth Arkansas Infantry raided the head of the sap opposite their position. While a party of Confederates created a diversionary action, McKennon and his men slipped up to within thirty yards of the sap, which was only about two hundred yards from the Confederate works. McKennon yelled, "Charge," and the Southerners swarmed into the work, taking seven prisoners, fourteen rifles, many sandbags, and killing or wounding several Yanks.[56] Gathering their plunder, the Arkansans withdrew to their lines, their loss but one soldier slightly wounded.

As the parallels drew closer and closer, the defenders of Port Hudson prepared for a last-ditch stand. After Captain Robert L. Pruyn returned from Jackson, Mississippi, on the night of June 26, the Southerners knew there was no hope of Johnston's relieving them. Two chances remained for the Confederates to defeat Banks—if General Dick Taylor could threaten New Orleans and panic Banks into retreating to defend that city,[57] or if Banks launched another major assault and was repulsed, the Army of the Gulf might well disintegrate as an effective military unit. Gardner had good information as to the next proposed assault. Confederate scouts in captured Yankee uniforms infiltrated Union lines and gleaned much intelligence from listening to Union officers talk.[58] Apparently even the lowest private inside Port Hudson knew about the thousand-man storming party. On June 22 a shocked Private Van Alstyne recorded in his diary: "The Rebs asked our pickets today when that thousand men was to come and get them." [59]

Inside the stronghold the supply of musket ammunition was virtually exhausted, and troops were detailed to pick up the Minié balls fired into Port Hudson by the enemy. The balls were melted, and the ordnance department manufactured 4,000 to 5,000 Enfield cartridges a day. Dud Yankee cannon shells were also collected. The projectiles which would fit Confederate guns were refixed by the ordnance men and fired right back at the Yanks. Many of the smaller shells which could not be used in the Confederate cannon were converted into hand grenades—a fire fuse being inserted in place of the detonator. The 8, 10, and 13-inch mortar shells which had failed to explode were dug up from the ground and converted into land torpedoes. Rows of these land mines were planted in front of Fort Desperate at night by Captain Louis Girard. The mines had friction primers attached, running inside Fort Desperate. If Federal troops advanced toward the Arkansans, engineer officers could explode the mines merely by pulling on the wires.[60]

Mortar shells were also planted in front of the Priest Cap.

Lieutenant Dabney and his men covered the outer edge of the parapet with hundreds of sharp wooden stakes—the points thrusting outward. Inside the Priest Cap was a crude *chevaux-de-frise,* and great numbers of artillery shells were planted with trip-wire fuses attached.[61] Stretches of piano wire were placed around the Priest Cap at heights of eighteen inches, so as to trip charging enemy soldiers.[62] As an added defense, the Mississippians constructed an interior line of works which the Federals could not mine. Similar defenses were constructed at the Citadel, with one important addition—a line of land mines was planted in the ditch outside the Citadel.

An interior line of earthworks was constructed behind the Citadel in case Union engineers succeeded in blowing Battery No. XI up. As the Federals' approaches grew nearer the Confederate defenses, Yank snipers began to pick off the Southerners as they went for water or supplies. In one instance, enemy sniping was so deadly that Gardner ordered a sortie. Troops from the Twelfth Arkansas made two attacks on the Yankee rifle pits, but were repulsed. Lieutenant Colonel E. C. Jordan, assuming command of the little force, drew his sword, took his cap in his left hand, and yelled, "Follow me, boys." [63] The enemy snipers were killed or captured, and Jordan and his little band returned to their lines in triumph.

As the last stage in Federal plans for the final assault, U.S. Army regulars erected a battery of Parrotts on the west bank of the Mississippi River, and Port Hudson was completely ringed in by Union cannon. On Friday morning, June 26, this new battery and every other battery the Federals possessed, plus the navy's heavy guns, commenced a tremendous bombardment, most of the fire being directed against the Citadel. Lieutenant L. A. Schirmer was directing the fire of the guns in Confederate Battery No. XI; despite his efforts, however, the battery was soon silenced by the heavy weight of Union metal. Cannon fire tore away the Confederate flag over the battery, which fell outside the works. Schirmer dashed out and seized the flag, "fixed it to a light pole, and, jumping on the parapet, planted the flag-staff amid a shower of bullets." Enemy fire repeatedly tore the flag down. But each time Schirmer put the "Stars and Bars" back up.[64]

Inside the Citadel, Confederate losses were light. Every day the parapet was breached by shell fire, and every night the damage was repaired under heavy blasts of grape and canister. On the night of June 29 the men of Miles' Legion, who had been holding the Citadel, were pulled to the left, being replaced by volunteers from the Eighteenth and Twenty-third Arkansas regiments, commanded by Colonel O. P. Lyles.[65] Before the Louisianians moved they had an unusual experience. Some of the Yanks fastened a rope to a dismounted gun inside the Citadel and tried to pull it out and down to their own lines. They could not budge it. The Federals then attempted to blow the gun up by throwing hand grenades at it; however, the fuses were too long and the Louisianians grabbed them and flung them back. The Zouaves, shocked as their own grenades burst in their faces, beat a hasty retreat down the slope of the hill, leaving behind one dead comrade.[66]

The following day, June 29, saw an attack on the Twelfth Arkansas, which held works to the left of the Citadel. Union soldiers began rolling bales of cotton toward the works, the attackers crouching behind the bales. Protected by the cotton, the Yankees had almost reached the edge of the parapet when the Confederates set the cotton ablaze by throwing firebrands. The discomfited Yanks withdrew to their works.[67]

On the night of June 29 Dwight's command launched an attack on the Citadel proper. Most of the Arkansans were not yet in position, and the bulk of the fight fell on the Louisianians and Lieutenant Wilkins' unattached company of Mississippians. The attack was made by the Sixth Michigan Infantry and the One Hundred Sixty-fifth New York Zouaves, both under the command of General Nickerson, who, according to Lieutenant Colonel Edward Bacon, "had prepared himself for it [the attack] by imbibing at the safe large quantities of the spirit of command." [68] Nickerson directed the attack from the shelter of the sap, his men moving out through the head of the sap and assaulting the Confederate position. With cries of "Give down!", the Yanks rushed the "Devil's Elbow." [69]

Spattering the Southerners with hand grenades, they leaped into the trenches, fighting with clubbed rifles. One Confederate was killed and four were captured. Private Charles Dustin, Company K, Sixth Michigan, made his way over the parapet and brought out a Confederate captain at bayonet point, turning his prisoner over to Captain Cordon.[70] The Federals were caught in a murderous cross fire and, according to one of their sergeants, "were repulsed in less time than it has taken me to write about it." [71] Sixteen Federals were killed and many more wounded in this brief but sanguinary engagement.

Their cannon dismounted, some of the men of De Gournay's Twelfth Louisiana Heavy Artillery Battalion were formed into a grenadier company. Armed with crude grenades, De Gournay's soldiers harassed the Union work parties in the head of the sap and in the gallery. The grenadiers would stand on the edge of the Devil's Elbow and "a stalwart artilleryman would take up one of the bombs, poise it over his right shoulder; the corporal standing behind would apply a light to the fuse and give the word, 'Let's go!' and the bomb, rolling down the chute, would fall and explode right in the faces or in the midst of the mining party." [72] Before the wooden chute was constructed from some old boards, the Confederates had been rolling shells down the slope, but the trough increased the accuracy of the attack.[73] Only the heavy shells were used in the chute, with the Louisianians throwing the smaller shells like hand grenades. Annoyed at having the heavy shells explode in their midst, the men of the Sixth Michigan sallied out and grabbed the end of the trough. A desperate tug of war followed. Other Michigan troops, Companies A and K, armed with Merrill breech-loading rifles, raked the Southerners with a murderous fire, and the trough was finally hauled into the Union sap.[74]

The Federals responded to the grenade attacks by hurling great numbers of small percussion hand grenades into the Confederate trenches at night. Usually the Southerners caught the grenades in their blankets and threw them back.[75] The grenades exploding in the Confederate trenches popped "like so many big firecrackers," waking the Confederates but causing few casualties.[76]

Grenade attacks took place at all points of the Port Hudson lines, and in front of the Priest Cap, Grover's men were forced to station watchmen to spot the grenades as they sailed through the air from the Confederate trenches. When the watchmen sang out that a grenade was coming, the Yanks would quickly retreat down the sap.[77] The artillery shells which the Confederates were throwing as grenades required fire fuses, and to prevent the Yanks from throwing them back before the fuses burned down, the Confederates cut the fuses short. Two of their own men from the First Mississippi were killed as a result of the grenades' exploding too soon.[78] The Yanks used some grenades with fire fuses, but they cut their fuses too long; consequently, the Confederates usually managed to throw them back.

Furious at the repulse of Nickerson's attacks, Dwight, from his headquarters at "the safe," ordered the luckless Sixth Michigan and the One Hundred Sixty-fifth New York to try again on the evening of June 30. With wild yells and reckless courage, the Yanks leaped over the ditch and swarmed up the parapet. Lyles's men held them at the parapet until gray reinforcements came up.[79] Driven back, many of the Yanks took shelter in the ditch, but they stepped on the land mines at the bottom of the ditch and were blown to pieces. The battered survivors fell back to their sap under cover of fire from Union artillery.[80]

The storming attacks having failed, Dwight's men resumed work on the sap and the mine, finishing them both about July 2. On July 3 the Federals started throwing up a large cavalier in front of the Citadel. Union artillery virtually blew away the exterior lunette which commanded a projecting ridge to the left of the position. The Union saps, mines, and cavaliers were virtually completed, and the army stood poised for another major assault. July 7 was set for the date of the assault. But the weather was bad, and Banks postponed it for forty-eight hours. This may well have been one of the decisive moments of the Civil War.

XI

The End

THE Army of the Gulf found itself in serious straits in late June and early July of 1863. The Federals had plenty of medicine, guns, ammunition, and food, but they were still in trouble. There was mutiny in the air. The officers and men were grimly dissatisfied. They had lost confidence in their generals. Officers of the One Hundred Seventy-third New York Infantry declared they would never go into battle again under Banks. Many officers were paying too much attention to the whisky bottle and not enough to the siege. Discipline was slack, and many soldiers wandered about without any duties to perform.[1] There apparently were two political cliques in the Federal army, the first being the old Butler group, consisting of the officers who had come to Louisiana with Butler and were closely associated with him. General Weitzel was the most prominent example. The second clique consisted of Banks's men—those who had come to Louisiana with the general in December, 1862, and who were considered loyal to him. The Banks clique was split by a division between the volunteer and regular officers. The volunteers felt that the West Pointers (regulars) had too much rank, and were undemocratic; and also, some of them were Democrats. Even Banks, as a former Democrat, was considered lacking in enthusiasm for the cause by some of the more ardent anti-slavery men.

The most immediate problem disrupting discipline was the disposition of the nine-month troops. The men of twenty of Banks's regiments at Port Hudson had enlisted for nine months and their terms of enlistment expired in mid or late June. In the May 27 and June 14 assaults the nine-month regiments suffered heavy losses, and many of the troops felt they were being unnecessarily sacrificed by Banks to save the lives of those of his men who belonged to the three-year regiments.[2] Banks claimed that the June 14 assault failed because the nine-month men refused to attack. He said, "The troops near the end of their enlistment say they do not feel like desperate service. The men enlisted for the war do not like to lead where the rest will not follow."[3] Relations between the nine-month and three-year troops were not particularly harmonious. In his diary Sergeant Solomon Nelson, Fiftieth Massachusetts, recorded that "it often happens to us nine-months men that a three-year one will ask us, as one did today, 'are you a soldier, or a nine-months man?' While resting in the shade he also sarcastically inquired why we did not take our bounty and buy a mule. We generously offered to buy him some soap if he would promise to use it on his person. This caused bad feelings, and we parted."[4]

The situation came to a head as the Fourth Massachusetts broke out in "open mutiny."[5] The mutineers claimed that their term of service had expired and "that they did not propose to be subjected to any further danger."[6] Banks wisely had the mutineers disarmed by loyal three-year troops. The regiment was deprived of its colors, several officers were publicly "stripped of the badges of their rank," and two companies were marched to the rear under heavy guard.[7] Some of the men of the Forty-eighth Massachusetts were also placed under arrest, and the men of the Fiftieth Massachusetts were close to mutiny. Banks tactfully informed the Fiftieth that if they mutinied they would be killed, or sent to the Dry Tortugas, which was almost the same thing.[8] In a desperate attempt to allay the situation, General Dudley addressed the regiment. "For God's sake boys," he told them, "don't rebel and make fools of yourselves, as a certain regiment has, and disgrace the old Bay State. Brace up; Port Hudson can't hold out long."[9] Stimulated by Dudley's plea and Banks's threat, the Fiftieth Massachusetts "volunteered" to stay another fourteen days.

The Forty-ninth Massachusetts was on the edge of mutiny, and its major went to Banks's headquarters on June 19 to try and determine the status of his men. Clerk Henry T. Johns remarked

Union fleet attempting to run past the Port Hudson batteries on March 14, 1863. In the lead is the *Hartford*, lashed to the gunboat *Albatross*. In the distant background is the doomed *Mississippi*.

Bluffs of Port Hudson, looking downriver. The fortified position at top left may be The Citadel.

Confederate gun position commanding the river. This was one of the smaller siege pieces at Port Hudson.

Union gun position firing on the Priest Cap. The cotton in the foreground came from bales used to protect the gunners.

A battery of heavy Union field guns. These guns were probably manned by the First Indiana Heavy Artillery.

Lone sentry stands atop a Confederate parapet. This photograph was probably taken after the siege ended.

Interior of The Citadel. The Confederates dug these holes to protect themselves from enemy fire.

Disabled Confederate field gun. Sandbagging was used to protect the men who worked these guns.

Interior of the Confederate works after Union bombardment. The gun in the foreground took a direct hit.

Key Confederate position known as the Priest Cap. The sharpened stakes were arranged to halt charging Union infantry.

of this visit: "I guess he learned there that if we refuse duty, we would have to measure arms with the power of the United States government." [10] The Forty-ninth remained loyal, but unrest continued. Sergeant Albert Plummer of the Forty-eighth Massachusetts wrote that on June 23 there was "considerable discussion of the vexing problem of termination of service." [11] There the matter ended.

The unrest among the Union army was not confined to nine-month troops, there being considerable muttering among the three-year men as to the competence of certain of their leaders. Dwight ordered the arrest of Lieutenant Colonel Bacon, Sixth Michigan, and Lieutenant Colonel Porter, Fourteenth Maine, for a lack of respect for their superior officers.[12] Bacon retaliated by writing a letter to Banks which contained a "concise statement of the crimes and absurdities of the siege." [13] He accused several generals of showing favoritism to staff officers, several officers of lying and cowardice, and Dwight of being a drunk. Dwight retaliated by writing a letter to Banks, asking that Bacon, Porter, and Colonel Kingman, Fifteenth New Hampshire, be summarily dismissed from the army for saying that the army's leaders were incompetent. Banks refused to act against the three officers, and the matter was dropped. But it was an indication of the disharmony existing within the ranks of the Union army.[14]

In addition to problems of mutiny and insubordination, Banks's worries were increased as Colonel Powers, with Stockdale's Mississippi Battalion, began slashing at his rear. At dawn on the morning of June 15 the Mississippians struck the camp of the Fourteenth New York Cavalry at Newport, two miles from Port Hudson. Many of the Yankees were asleep; others were out picking blackberries for breakfast as the Mississippians galloped up and took the whole bunch prisoner without firing a shot. Some of the Mississippians then attacked Company C, Third Massachusetts Cavalry, which was on picket duty. The Yankees broke under the wild charge, and "there was not the slightest hesitancy on the part of any" at retreating.[15] They fled for two miles—until they reached the rest of the army and protection of the artillery. Despite all the lead the Confederates threw, only one

Federal, Private William Dane, was killed. At the same time, four of Stockdale's men captured the infantry guard at the Carter house, which was being used as a hospital. Not a shot was fired as the Yankees surrendered in the face of an "overwhelming force" of numbers.[16]

Before the Federals could counterattack, Powers and Stockdale were gone from Newport, reaching their base at Freeman's plantation a few hours later. Eight hundred sabers, eight wagons and teams, sixteen hundred pistols, and much ammunition were taken, besides all of Companies A, C, F, and G, as well as most of Company E.[17]

The Newport raid added to Banks's worries, and in desperation he ordered barricades thrown up across the roads leading into Port Hudson in order to prevent Logan from charging in and routing his army some dark night. With so much concentration on barricading the roads, Banks forgot to make preparations to prevent Logan's men from charging across the fields.[18]

Even with Logan's cavalry lurking in the rear, Banks decided to send out a foraging expedition of 140 wagons to the nearby town of Jackson, with the Fifty-second Massachusetts Infantry, One Hundred Fourteenth New York Infantry, two field pieces, and a body of Grierson's cavalry as guards. The force reached Jackson without incident, but as the soldiers began looting the farms, houses, and barns, their work was suddenly interrupted by the sharp crack of rifle fire. In the words of Corporal James K. Hosmer, "The Philistines were upon us." The Yankee pickets came galloping into the main body, with Confederate cavalrymen in hot pursuit. The "contraband" drivers panicked at the sight of the graycoated cavalrymen, and a scene of the wildest confusion ensued. The mule teams pulling the wagons, many without drivers, broke into full gallop, running "over ditches and fences, crashing through groves of young pines, over logs and stumps. . . . The negro drivers yelled, and brandished their whips." [19] Only a stand by the Union artillery held the Confederates back, enabling the Yanks to retire toward Port Hudson. The retreat was not uneventful. Logan's raiders caught up with the column and "swept like a whirlwind" through the long, straggling line, capturing sixty wagons and many drivers. Again the only thing preventing disaster for the Federals was the fire from their two cannon, which swept the Southerners back.[20]

On June 23 a seven-man patrol raided Cedar Grove plantation near Jackson, behaving "like thieves," but the Yankees "seemed to be frightened" and did not stay long.[21] Meanwhile, during the time the Union soldiers were raiding private homes, Logan's cavalry was out for bigger game. In late June, Confederate sympathizers informed Colonel Logan that General Neal Dow was convalescing at the Heath plantation, only two miles from Port Hudson. Captain John McKowen, home on leave from Virginia, contacted Mrs. Heath, who agreed to help him capture her uninvited guest. On the night of June 30 McKowen and two of Logan's scouts slipped through some boards in the Heath back fence which Mrs. Heath had arranged for a servant to loosen. Yankee sentries patrolled the house and grounds, but the three raiders were able to enter the back door of the house without interference. Inside, Mrs. Heath guided the Confederates to her guest's bedroom. She had earlier oiled the hinges of the door, so that there was no telltale squeak as Captain McKowen opened the door and quietly slipped in, a cocked pistol in his hand. Walking over to the sleeping general's bed, McKowen aimed his revolver at Dow's face and shook him. Through sleep-clouded eyes, Dow saw the barrel of the gun pointing at his face and heard a voice whispering, "One word, and you are a dead man! Make no noise. Come with us!" Within seconds Dow was dressed and en route to Logan's headquarters, as a prisoner of war, eventually to be exchanged for General W. H. F. "Rooney" Lee, second son of General Robert E. Lee, who had been wounded at Brandy Station and captured while convalescing.[22]

Logan followed up Dow's capture with a raid on Banks's supply center at Springfield Landing. On July 2, about 8:30 A.M., two hundred troopers, split into three parties, attacked and routed the picket of the One Hundred Sixty-second New York, stationed on the old Springfield road, and then rode down the road to the landing, routing a party of thirty Negroes belonging to Daniel Ullman's brigade. The Confederates were provided with bottles of turpentine and matches, and within seconds the great heaps of Union quartermaster supplies at the landing were in flame. The first raiding party then attacked the administration buildings, but the Yankees fled aboard the steamer *Suffolk,* which put out into the stream and safety. The provost guard from the Sixteenth New Hampshire made a stand from behind the levee, emptying several Confederate saddles. The second raiding party attacked the "contrabands' huts" located in the rear of the cottonwood grove on the right of the road, stampeding the Negroes into a wild panic.[23] The Confederates were shelled by a Yankee gunboat, probably the *Suffolk,* which was armed,[24] but the third raiding party hit the post commissary anyway. The One Hundred Sixty-second New York arrived and forced the Confederates to retreat "in some confusion." The Southerners reformed on the plank road after capturing the Yankee pickets and retired to Freeman's plantation.[25] Logan reported that he had destroyed a hundred wagons and inflicted heavy losses on the garrison, and that his own loss was four killed and ten wounded.[26]

Clashes between Logan's and Grierson's commands continued. On July 4 a skirmish occurred at the Fluker house near Jackson in which one Yankee was killed and at least one captured. On July 7 Logan's scouts took six prisoners near Port Hudson. Union cavalry operating from Baton Rouge, attempting to divert Confederate attention from Grierson, also brought on several clashes. On the Amite road a Union patrol from Baton Rouge was ambushed, and one non-commissioned officer was taken prisoner by the Southerners. Another officer was severely wounded.[27]

Logan's cavalry failed to make any major assaults on Banks's rear, and inside Port Hudson the situation was rapidly worsening. "We are still in good health and spirits," W. C. Porter, a member of the Sixteenth Arkansas wrote in his diary on July 4.[28] Although spirits were good, the Confederates' stomachs were empty. The supply of mule, horse, dog, and rat meat was not inexhaustible, but the Southerners were willing to fight on, unaware of the events occurring elsewhere that were to make the fall of Port Hudson a certainty.

In Mississippi, General Joseph E. Johnston's army failed to relieve Vicksburg, and on July 4, 1863, General Pemberton was forced to yield to Grant, who immediately made preparations to send reinforcements to Banks. In the early hours of Tuesday, July 7, the gunboat *General Price* reached Port Hudson, bringing the news that Vicksburg, the "Gibraltar of the West," had surrendered. Colonel Kilby Smith of Grant's staff personally delivered the news to Banks at 10.45 A.M.[29] The news was soon communicated to the Union soldiers in the trenches, and a "surging volume of cheers and exultations filled the air all along the lines around Port Hudson."[30] A Yankee colonel wrapped his official copy of the news around a stick and hurled it into the Confederate trenches. Banks issued a general order calling for a salute of a hundred shotted guns to be fired, and at noon the Nineteenth Army Corps's musicians filled the air with Union melodies. Union troops shouted to the Confederates the news of Vicksburg, but the Southerners thought it was a *ruse de guerre*. An Arkansas officer shouted back to the Yanks, "This is another damned Yankee lie!"[31] An official copy of Grant's dispatch to Banks was brought through the lines by some pickets and delivered to General Gardner, who was seated on the portico at his headquarters smoking a pipeful of magnolia blossoms. Gardner was visibly upset by the intelligence and instructed Captain Crawford Jackson to issue a call for his senior officers to meet at headquarters immediately.[32]

That night Gardner, Beall, Steedman, Miles, Lyles, Shelby, and Marshall Smith held a council of war. It was obvious to these officers that Banks would not launch another attack, there being no need for it. The Yanks could simply sit in their trenches until the Southerners were starved into surrendering.[33] There no longer being any practical reason for holding Port Hudson, the council decided that it would be well to seek terms with Banks, and for this purpose Gardner immediately entered into negotiations with the head of the besieging army. About 12:30 A.M. on July 8 a cease-fire was arranged along the Plains Store road and a Confederate officer delivered a message to Colonel Charles J. Paine's headquarters. Lieutenant Orton S. Clark then transmitted the

message to Banks's headquarters. Banks opened the envelope
and found that Gardner was asking for official confirmation of
Pemberton's surrender. Banks replied by sending a courier into
Confederate lines with an official copy of the Vicksburg surrender. Upon reading the message, Gardner asked to discuss the
question of surrendering Port Hudson with a commission of
Union officers. A conference was arranged to meet at 9 A.M.,
and Banks designated General Charles P. Stone, Colonel Henry
W. Birge, and Lieutenant Colonel Richard B. Irwin as his commissioners.[34] All firing ceased, and at the appointed hour the
Confederate commissioners, together with Steedman, Miles, and
Smith, went out to meet the Yankees. The two groups met in a
tent between the lines. The Federals wanted an immediate surrender; the Southerners tried to delay things until some of their
men could escape through Union lines.[35] Negotiations began at
9 A.M., but it was after 2 P.M. before the articles were signed by
both Gardner and Banks. In view of the lateness of the hour,
the Yankees agreed to postpone the surrender ceremony until
the next morning. (This delay was exactly what the Confederates
wanted, so that any of the Confederates who wished to escape
might do so during the night.) Around 3 P.M. the Federals sent
a wagon train of food and drugs into Port Hudson.[36]

The Confederates stuffed themselves with the good Yankee
food, and as darkness fell many of these men and officers commenced escape attempts. Captain Pruyn, who had already made
two trips through the Union lines during the siege, swam down
the Mississippi River, followed by Ben Burnett of the Fourth
Louisiana. Both men escaped. Three other members of the
Fourth, the Clark brothers, made crude floats from numerous
empty canteens and followed Pruyn and Burnett a few hours
later.[37] Captain Crawford Jackson made a daring escape by
galloping through the lines, posing as a Union officer on special
duty. A Federal officer eyed him suspiciously, but Jackson sa-
luted and in a second the officer ordered, "Open ranks men, and
let that officer pass." [38] After several close calls, Jackson made
it to Clinton, and then to Osyka, Mississippi.

Many Confederate officers slipped through the Union lines

by crawling on their hands and knees, taking the great risk of being killed. Lieutenants E. J. M. Padgett and William F. Clements spent three days and nights working their way through the lines. They suffered severely from thirst, but reached safety. The two were picked up by Logan's cavalrymen and were nearly shot as Yank spies before proving their identity.[39] Major Samuel L. Knox and other officers and men of the First Alabama hid near the outer lines and crawled out to safety on the night of July 9.[40] Lieutenant Colonel Lee of the Fifteenth Arkansas and Captain Hardee of Miles' Legion were not so fortunate; they were captured by members of the Thirteenth Connecticut. Captain Homer Sprague of that regiment related that he gave the two half-starved officers a meal, furnished Captain Hardee "with a copious supply of whiskey," and sent the two officers on to General Grover under guard.[41]

As the sun rose on the morning of July 9 the Confederates who had not escaped during the night lined up to officially surrender. At 7 A.M. the Union occupation column entered the Jackson road sally-port, General Andrews heading the column, followed by Birge's storming party and other outstanding Federal units. Andrews and Gardner conferred for a few moments, and Gardner offered him his sword, saying, "Having thoroughly defended this position as long as I deemed it necessary, I now surrender to you my sword, and with it this post and this garrison." Andrews replied, "I return your sword as a proper compliment to the gallant commander of such gallant troops—conduct that would be heroic in another cause." [42] Kissing the hilt of the sword,[43] he returned the blade to the Confederate commander, who sheathed it and replied to the Federal officer, "This is neither the time nor the place to discuss the cause." [44]

At 9:30 A.M. General Beall turned to the members of his command and ordered, "Attention! Ground arms!" The Southerners placed their weapons on the ground with a considerable lack of enthusiasm, their mood being, "We shall meet you again. This is not the last of us." [45] From the Confederate ranks mutterings were heard: "Damn you! You couldn't take us by fighting! You had to starve us out." [46] In the words of one Union observer, "The expressions on their faces and glances from their eyes . . . disclosed the fact that hatred of the North had not surrendered its throne in their hearts." [47]

After the surrender ceremonies Banks decided to parole the enlisted men and promised to parole the officers in a few days. And he agreed to allow the Confederate officers to retain their side arms. By July 14 or 15 the Confederate enlisted men and non-commissioned officers were on their way home, their sick and wounded carried on horses, mules, and wagons, except for about five hundred who were left behind for the Union army to care for.[48] Banks committed a serious error in paroling the men because Gardner was the only Confederate officer with authority to approve the paroles, and as a prisoner himself, he could not legally do so.[49]

Outraged by what they considered Southern perfidy, the Northerners charged the Confederates with violations of the rules of warfare when the Davis government declared the paroles null and void. General Halleck admitted that the paroles were not arranged in accordance with the Seventh Article of the cartel then in effect with the Confederate government.[50] The enlisted men were furloughed by the Confederate government and ordered to report to Chattanooga, Tennessee; Demopolis, Alabama; Enterprise, Mississippi, or Morton, Mississippi, by September 15. The troops were immediately reorganized and soon were seeing active duty against the Federals.

About half of the Port Hudson officers were sent to Johnson's Island prison camp, in Ohio, where many died from disease. Some Confederate officers were reportedly murdered while at this camp.[51] The remaining officers from Port Hudson were sent to New Orleans and imprisoned at the United States Customs House on Canal Street or in warehouses around Port Street. Many escaped from Union custody, eventually rejoining their units.[52]

Some controversy surrounds the exact size and losses of the two armies at Port Hudson. Records show that on May 19 Gardner had 4,652 men present for duty at or near Port Hudson, and an aggregate present of 5,715.[53] Between May 21 and June 1 the Confederate garrison lost 80 killed, 230 wounded, and 96 missing.[54] Gardner's June 30 returns show that 2,803 men were present for duty, with an aggregate present of 4,098, and an absolute total of 6,273 men absent and present, including the sick, wounded, missing, armed civilians, cooks, clerks, teamsters, and staff officers.[55] When Port Hudson fell on July 9, 1863, the Federals paroled 5,935 men, including civilian employees.[56] Four hundred and five Confederate officers were not paroled and were sent as prisoners of war to New Orleans or Memphis, thence to permanent prisoner of war camps. The total strength of the garrison, counting those paroled, those retained as prisoners, killed, dead from disease, or escaped, would thus seem to be about 6,800 men, including civilians. From May 21 to the surrender the garrison lost 188 killed and 483 wounded—a total of 671 men, in addition to about 200 men who died from sickness.[57]

Union Army of the Gulf casualties totaled 752 killed, 226 mortally wounded, 3,228 wounded, and 418 captured or missing. In addition to the ships' crews of Farragut and Porter, 30,000 to 40,000 United States soldiers served at Port Hudson between May 23 and July 9, 1863.[58] No reliable figures have been preserved to show the exact number of troops available on any given day. There were constant losses in the Union ranks from Confederate fire and the hot Louisiana climate. More than 4,700, and probably as many as 5,200 men were actual battle casualties, and over 4,000 soldiers were hospitalized from sunstroke or disease, including a great number of Union officers. The army consisted of sixty-one regiments—fifty-four infantry, five cavalry, one engineer, and one heavy artillery. There were also thirteen field batteries and one section of a fourteenth attached to the infantry division.[59]

The nine-month regiments had an average organized enlistment strength of 908 men.[60] These regiments had arrived in Louisiana in December, 1862, and although suffering few casualties from Confederate actions, did lose many men from the Louisiana climate. A majority of the men from more than half the regiments were soon taken sick. Some of the sick Yankees died; others were sent home, but most of them were soon able to return to their regiments. The average strength of the nine-month regiments at Port Hudson, as of May 23, was probably over 600. On June 30, after five weeks of fighting, the Twenty-eighth Connecticut numbered 502 men present for duty, and an aggregate present of 565.[61] The three-year regiments, which had come to Louisiana with Butler, were nearly at full strength. Heavy losses from the climate had been incurred at first, but after a year in Louisiana the Federals were thoroughly acclimated. The Eighth Vermont Infantry had been mustered in with a strength of 1,060 men, and started its part in the siege of Port Hudson with 940 men present for duty.[62] The Eighth and other Butler regiments were bolstered up by the arrival of drafts of replacements from the North—as were a few of Banks's regiments—and were up to 88 per cent of original fighting strength. Assuming that the Butler regiments were of approximately the same strength and received the same number of replacements, their average strength was probably above 800 men per regiment at the beginning of the siege. Banks's three-year regiments, recruited in the summer and fall of 1862, originally numbered about 1,000 men each—the One Hundred Fifty-ninth New York was mustered in with 840 men.[63] These regiments, having in many cases seen arduous service, probably reached Port Hudson with around 500 men each. The five infantry regiments of the Corps d'Afrique mustered about 1,400 effectives at Port Hudson.[64] The First Louisiana regiment of engineers, under Colonel Justin Hodge, mustered 1,000 men, of whom 800 were fit for duty in the trenches.[65]

The "Tri-monthly Returns for May," issued from Banks's headquarters, show that the army before Port Hudson on May 31 numbered 31,261 officers and men present for duty. The same returns indicate that there was an aggregate present of 37,392 men, and a total of 49,365 present and absent. These returns exclude the garrison along the Opelousas Railroad and Brashear City, but probably include the Baton Rouge and Butte à la Rose commands.[66] One month later, June 30, a second set of returns was compiled at the headquarters of the Nineteenth Army Corps before Port Hudson. In the intervening thirty days the casualty reports from the May 27 battle were turned in to headquarters, although in many cases these returns were incomplete. The battle of June 14 took place and the casualty reports for this action were also collected, as were the reports for the numerous minor operations occuring during the month. Strong reinforcements, numbering many thousands of soldiers, arrived to bolster Banks's army, but after June 20 several units had to be sent to Donaldsonville to strengthen the garrison there. The June 30 "Tri-monthly Returns" show that 22,962 men were present for duty at Port Hudson. This return also shows there was an aggregate present of 28,403 men, and a total of 43,105 men present and absent.[67] This report excludes the garrisons at New Orleans and Baton Rouge. Butte a la Rose had been evacuated and the garrison at Brashear City had been captured by the Confederates on June 23. The Donaldsonville garrison was under General W. H. Emory's New Orleans command.[68]

The difference between the May 31 and June 30 returns is 8,399. This is approximately the number of men the Nineteenth Army Corps lost in this period from all causes—killed, wounded, missing, captured, or hospitalized at Baton Rouge and New Orleans from sunstroke and disease. The forces which Banks sent to reinforce Donaldsonville were more than offset by the reinforcements the Army of the Gulf before Port Hudson received.[69]

Banks was aided in the siege by Federal naval forces under Farragut, whose ships' crews probably numbered over 2,000 men. The armored *Essex* reported six wounded, and the wooden ships suffered losses, but there are no complete casualty returns for the naval forces in the siege. Banks's army employed thousands of slave laborers as teamsters, workers, cooks, and servants. Clerk Henry Johns said, "Darkeys are so abundant that nearly every man . . . keeps his waiter." [70] Many of the contrabands working in the trenches were killed by Confederate fire, but their losses were never counted in the official returns.

In terms of casualties, the Confederates won the siege of Port Hudson. Union combat losses ran around 5,000 as against about 700 Confederates, roughly seven to one in favor of the South. About 200 Confederate soldiers lost their lives from disease, but over 4,000 Northerners were hospitalized from disease. Many of them died. The only other permanent Confederate casualties were the 405 officers taken prisoner at the surrender, and many of these eventually escaped. The Union troops were disheartened by the siege and some of the nine-month troops refused to re-enlist at the close of the siege, thus adding to the permanent Federal losses.

The two men who sealed the fate of Port Hudson—Banks and Gardner—demonstrated unusual qualities of tactical ability during the siege. Banks's plans of operations, original and daring in concept, should have brought about the fall of Port Hudson many weeks earlier. But Banks was completely inept at executing his plans. The timing of the attacks on May 27 and June 14 was fantastically poor—the intervals between the assaults sometimes lasting several hours—allowing the Confederates to mass troops at threatened points along their lines. The Union commander was extremely careless about reconnoitering the ground over which the attacks were to be made. Soldiers often charged forward at the Southerners, only to get tangled up, and sometimes even lost, in the mazes of tangled ravines, gullies, creek bottoms, crevasses, chopped-down trees, and thick foliage which protected the exterior of the Confederate works. On May 27, and again in the June 14 assault, Banks displayed understanding of the modern tactics coming into vogue by his use of heavy skirmish lines—employing the equivalent of an infantry brigade solely as skirmishers. And Banks was aggressive, hard-hitting, courageous, and stubborn. But he was hopelessly handicapped by his lack of practical military knowledge and by the collection of incompetent subordinate officers with which he surrounded himself. Many critics declared he "failed seriously in developing a co-ordinated assault on May 27," [71] but part of the blame must fall on some of his subordinate officers for failing to work together. His generals spent too much time stealing cotton, drinking whisky, or persuading their troops to take temperance pledges, and not enough serious time at planning how to defeat the Confederates.[72] One possible explanation of Banks's weak behavior in dealing with his subordinates is that he "seriously expected to be President of the United States some day," and hesitated to anger potential allies like Dwight and others.[73] An opinion of Union generalship expressed by some of the Yankee soldiers was: "We are poorly led and uselessly slaughtered, and the brains are all within and not 'before Port Hudson.'" [74]

Gardner, much more competent at handling troops than Banks, lacked his opponent's aggressiveness and reckless determination to win. West Point trained, Gardner was a highly competent engineer and organizer who was able to thoroughly coordinate the Confederate defenses. While the Union army fought the siege by individual brigades and divisions, Gardner worked the Confederates like a smooth, well-oiled machine—each unit doing the right thing at the right time. The greatest Southern weakness was the lack of provisions, troops, and fire power; yet, Gardner shrewdly offset these disadvantages by employing modern military tactics and devices of war. To increase his fire power and to supplement the scanty number of line troops, each Confederate soldier was equipped with one or more captured rifles and several smoothbore muskets or shotguns. By using homemade buckshot cartridges in their smoothbores (flintlocks and percussions), the Confederates were able to turn their inferior arms into weapons that were superior to the modern Yankee rifles at close range.[75] Another means of increasing fire power, at the Citadel and the Priest Cap, was the bracing-up of the wrecked Confederate cannon on blocks. These guns were loaded with "bags of all sorts of scrap iron which were to be fired in the face of a storming party." [76]

Gardner displayed great imagination in allowing his staff of young engineer officers to direct the powerful inner defensive system which consisted of land mines, *chevaux de frise,* inner lines of works, and countermines. One outstanding characteristic of Gardner's defense was that he insisted on maintaining a strategic reserve at all times to be used in case of emergency, despite the desperate shortage of troops. The worst criticism of Gardner's defense of the garrison was that it was almost completely passive, there being only a few minor sorties against the Federals. After the May 27 attack, and especially after the June 14 assault,

Gardner had excellent opportunities to sally out and hurt Banks's army severely. In the battle at the Priest Cap on the morning of June 14, less than six hundred Confederate soldiers were closely engaged, and after 10 A.M. Gardner could easily have collected sufficient fresh troops to counterattack Weitzel and Birge. He failed to attack, and a possible opportunity for lifting the siege was lost.

Even though Gardner failed to attack Banks and attempt to break the siege, even though Gardner lost Port Hudson, the immutable truth remains that he and his little band of Confederates put up one of the best fights of the war, turning Port Hudson into a slaughterhouse for the troops of the United States Nineteenth Army Corps. The Yankees took Port Hudson, but they paid a terrible price in blood. The history books merely enter the record of the Port Hudson struggle as "Vicksburg having fallen, Port Hudson surrendered"—a brief way of disposing of a chapter in American history in which the actors on both sides demonstrated a devotion and endurance that should rank high in the annals of that tragedy which we now call the Civil War.

Appendix I

THE PORT HUDSON GARRISON MAY 23–JULY 9, 1863

Maj. Gen. Franklin Gardner

INFANTRY

First Alabama—Lt. Col. M. B. Locke (w), Maj. S. L. Knox
Forty-ninth Alabama—Maj. T. A. Street
First Mississippi—Lt. Col. A. S. Hamilton
Thirty-ninth Mississippi—Col. W. B. Shelby
Claiborne Light Infantry—Capt. G. W. Lewis
Natchez Light Infantry—Lt. Wilkins (k), Lt. Chase (k)
First Arkansas Battalion—Lt. Col. B. Jones
Tenth Arkansas—Col. Witt (c), Col. E. L. Vaughan
Twelfth Arkansas—Col. T. J. Reid
Fifteenth Arkansas—Col. Ben W. Johnson
Sixteenth Arkansas—Col. David Provence
Eighteenth Arkansas—Col. Parish
Twenty-third Arkansas—Col. O. P. Lyles
Miles' Louisiana Legion—Col. W. R. Miles
Ninth Louisiana Battalion—Maj. B. R. Chinn
Infantry detachments from *Fourth Louisiana*—Capt. Charles T. Whitman
Infantry detachments from *Thirtieth Louisiana*—Capt. T. K. Porter
Special Improvised Tennessee Battalion (details from *Forty-first, Forty-second, Forty-eighth, Forty-ninth, Fifty-third* and *Fifty-fifth Tennessee*)—Capt. S. A. Whiteside

127

ARTILLERY

Company B, First Tennessee Light Artillery—Capt. F. J. Weller (k)
Company G, First Tennessee Light Artillery—Capt. J. A. Fisher (k)
Watson's Louisiana Battery—Lt. E. A. Toledano
Twelfth Louisiana Heavy Artillery Battery—Lt. Col. P. F. De Gournay
First Alabama Heavy Artillery Battalion
Batteries B, F, and K, First Mississippi Field Artillery—Capts. A. J. Herod, J. L. Bradford, and George Abbay
English Battery—Capt. J. T. English
Seven Stars Battery—Lt. F. W. Coleman

CAVALRY

Wingfield's Ninth Louisiana Partisan Battalion

Total Confederate losses, including known cavalry casualties: 188 killed, 483 wounded, 200 dead from disease or sunstroke.

Appendix II

ARMY OF THE GULF, U.S.A. (NINETEENTH ARMY CORPS)
Maj. Gen. N. P. Banks

FIRST DIVISION—Maj. Gen. C. C. Augur
First Brigade—Col. E. P. Chapin (k), Col. Charles J. Paine; Second Louisiana, Twenty-first Maine, Forty-eighth Massachusetts, Forty-ninth Massachusetts, One Hundred Sixteenth New York
Second Brigade—Col. N. A. M. Dudley; Thirtieth Massachusetts, Fiftieth Massachusetts, One Hundred Sixty-first New York, One Hundred Seventy-fourth New York
Artillery—First Indiana Heavy, Col. J. A. Keith; First Maine Battery, Sixth Massachusetts Battery, Twelfth Massachusetts (I section), Eighteenth New York, Battery A, First U.S.; Battery G, Fifth U.S.

SECOND DIVISION—Brig. Gen. T. W. Sherman (w), Brig. Gen. W. M. Dwight
First Brigade—Brig. Gen. Neal Dow (w), Col. D. S. Cowles (k), Col. T. S. Clark; Twenty-sixth Connecticut, Sixth Michigan, Fifteenth New Hampshire, One Hundred Twenty-eighth New York, One Hundred Sixty-second New York
Third Brigade—Brig. Gen. F. S. Nickerson; Fourteenth Maine, Twenty-fourth Maine, Twenty-eighth Maine, One Hundred Sixty-fifth New York, One Hundred Seventy-fifth New York, One Hundred Seventy-seventh New York
Artillery Batteries—Twenty-first New York, First Vermont

129

THIRD DIVISION—Brig. Gen. Halbert E. Paine (w), Col. Hawkes Fearing, Jr.

First Brigade—Col. Samuel P. Farris; Sixteenth New Hampshire, Twenty-eighth Connecticut, Fourth Massachusetts, One Hundred Tenth New York

Second Brigade—Maj. John H. Allcot; Eighth New Hampshire, One Hundred Thirty-third New York, One Hundred Seventy-third New York, Fourth Wisconsin

Third Brigade—Col. Oliver P. Gooding; Thirty-first Massachusetts, Thirty-eighth Massachusetts, Fifty-third Massachusetts, One Hundred Fifty-sixth New York

Artillery Batteries—Fourth Massachusetts; Battery F, First U.S.; Second Vermont

FOURTH DIVISION—Brig. Gen. Cuvier Grover

First Brigade—Col. R. E. Holcomb (k), Col. Joseph S. Morgan; First Louisiana, Twenty-second Maine, Ninetieth New York, Ninety-first New York, One Hundred Thirty-first New York

Second Brigade—Col. William K. Kimball; Twenty-fourth Connecticut, Twelfth Maine, Fifty-second Massachusetts

Third Brigade—Col. H. W. Birge; Thirteenth Connecticut, Twenty-fifth Connecticut, Twenty-sixth Maine, One Hundred Fifty-ninth New York

Artillery Batteries—Second Massachusetts; Battery L, First U.S.; Battery C, Second U.S.

Corps d'Afrique—Brig. Gen. Daniel Ullman; Sixth, Seventh, Eighth, Ninth, Tenth Infantry

Cavalry—Col. Benjamin H. Grierson; Sixth Illinois, Seventh Illinois, First Louisiana, Third Massachusetts, Fourteenth New York (six companies)

Total Union Army losses: 752 killed, 226 known mortally wounded, 3,228 wounded, and 418 captured or missing, plus over 4,000 hospitalized from disease or sunstroke. These figures are not complete. Union casualty returns as reported in *Official Records* are, for the most part, in error, apparently because of the heavy officer casualties and the resulting confusion in keeping records.

Notes

CHAPTER I · *Prelude*

1   See Charles L. Dufour, *The Night the War Was Lost* (Garden City, 1960), 326–30.
2   Benson J. Lossing, *Pictorial History of the Civil War in the United States of America* (Hartford, 1869), II, 598.
3   Thomas P. Kettell, *History of the Great Rebellion* (San Francisco, 1863), II, 750.
4   Milledge L. Bonham, Jr., "Man and Nature at Port Hudson," *Military Historian and Economist,* II (1917), 372. The site of Port Hudson is no longer on the river. The Mississippi has moved away from it.
5   Daniel P. Smith, *Company K, First Alabama Regiment, Three Years in the Confederate Service* (Prattville, Ala., 1885), 40.
6   Lieutenant Howard C. Wright, *Port Hudson: Its History From an Interior Point of View* (Baton Rouge, 1961), 10. This valuable account by a Confederate officer was originally published in the New Orleans *Daily True Delta* soon after the surrender of the Port Hudson garrison.
7   Lossing, *Pictorial History of the Civil War,* 598.
8   Harry Bates Brown, Jr., "Port Hudson: A Study in Historical Geography" (M.A. Thesis, Louisiana State University, 1936), 59.
9   H. Skipwith, *East Feliciana, Louisiana: Past and Present* (New Orleans, 1892), 66.
10   Brown, "Port Hudson," 58.
11   Smith, *Company K, First Alabama Regiment,* 40.

CHAPTER II · *River Bastion*

1   New Orleans *Times-Democrat,* April 26, 1906. Reverend J. H. McNeilly said there were but "slight" fortifications at the time of the fall of New Orleans. McNeilly, a chaplain at Port Hudson until May, 1863, was with the Forty-ninth Tennessee Infantry. See *Confederate Veteran,* XXVII (1919), 337.
2   New Orleans *Times-Democrat,* April 26, 1906.
3   *The War of the Rebellion: A Compilation of the Official Records of the Union and Confederate Armies* (Washington, 1800–1901),

Ser. I, Vol. XV, 794. Hereinafter cited as *Official Records* (unless otherwise indicated, all citations are to Series I).

4   *Ibid.,* 800.

5   *Ibid.,* 794.

6   *Confederate Veteran,* XII (1904), 405. At the beginning of the war De Gournay was on the staff of the New Orleans *Picayune.* When the fighting broke out, he equipped at his own expense a company of artillery, of which he was captain.

7   *Official Records,* XV, 800.

8   *Ibid.,* 81.

9   *Ibid.,* 804.

10 *Harper's Pictorial History of the Civil War* (New York, 1869), 460.

11 *Official Records of the Union and Confederate Navies in the War of the Rebellion* (Washington, 1905), XIX, 180–84; Dunbar Rowland, *The Official and Statistical Register of the State of Mississippi* (Nashville, 1908), 851; *Harper's Pictorial History,* 460.

12 Wright, *Port Hudson,* 8. Porter's report is in *Official Records of the Union and Confederate Navies,* XIX, 182. According to De Gournay, the Confederates had one heavy Parrott rifle and two 12-pound field pieces. He said that the fire from the *Essex* killed one mule "peacefully grazing in a field beyond our lines." *Confederate Veteran,* XIII (1905), 31–32.

13 Sarah Morgan Dawson, *A Confederate Girl's Diary* (Bloomington, 1960), 236–37.

14 Wright, *Port Hudson,* 6.

15 John R. Spears, *History of the United States Navy* (London, 1898), IV, 78.

16 *Official Records,* XV, 846; Smith, *Company K, First Alabama Regiment,* 40. Smith stated that there were fourteen or fifteen guns mounted, including an 8-inch gun and a 10-inch Columbiad. *Confederate Veteran,* X (1902), 365, stated that two of the 32-pound guns had been taken from the Union gunboat *Sumter* by Lieutenant F. M. Mumford, who, with a small force of Louisiana troops, had bluffed the Northerners into surrendering at Bayou Sara.

17 *Official Records,* XV, 809, 844–46. Captain R. M. Boone's battery was located about four hundred yards from Troth's Landing. This was in order to oppose a Federal landing at the spot, which was about three miles below Port Hudson.

18 *Ibid.,* 804.

19 *Ibid.,* 841. A complete list of units is given on this page.

20 Rowland, *Official and Statistical Register,* 722; *Official Records,* XV, 843.
21 Smith, *Company K, First Alabama Regiment,* 39. Ezra J. Warner, *Generals in Gray, Lives of the Confederate Commanders* (Baton Rouge, 1959), simply states that Villepigue fell victim to fever. F. Jay Taylor (ed.), *Reluctant Rebel: The Secret Diary of Robert Patrick 1861–1865* (Baton Rouge, 1959), 53, states that Villepigue died at the Gibbons house where he was quartered, "of typhoid pneumonia."
22 Smith, *Company K, First Alabama Regiment,* 44. Off-duty troops sometimes made candles and soap. Some of them drank Louisiana rum, which sold at a dollar a glass. J. P. Cannon, *Inside of Rebeldom: The Daily Life of a Private in the Confederate Army* (Washington, 1900), 74, 76, 89. The more adventuresome Confederates went fishing in the Mississippi River, or sneaked off with their guns and hunted alligators. J. V. Frederick (ed.), "War Diary of W. C. Porter," *Arkansas Historical Quarterly,* XVIII (1952), 305.
23 *Confederate Veteran,* XXVII (1919), 337.
24 *Ibid.*
25 *Ibid.*
26 Cannon, *Inside of Rebeldom,* 77.
27 *Confederate Veteran,* XXVII (1919), 337.
28 Smith, *Company K, First Alabama Regiment,* 45. Some of the troops made crude mattresses of Spanish moss. Cannon, *Inside of Rebeldom,* 72.
29 Dawson, *A Confederate Girl's Diary,* 234.
30 Taylor (ed.), *Secret Diary of Robert Patrick,* 57; Smith, *Company K, First Alabama Regiment,* 44.
31 Smith, *Company K, First Alabama Regiment,* 45; *Official Records of the Union and Confederate Navies,* XIX, 408; Taylor (ed.), *Secret Diary of Robert Patrick,* 63. Patrick gives a somewhat lurid version of the action at Profit Island, which appears in his account as "Prophet's Island."

CHAPTER III · *The Campaign Begins*

1 This was a political nickname applied to Banks. As a boy his job had been to remove full bobbins from the spring frames of the Boston Manufacturing Company. Fred Harvey Harrington, *Fighting Politician: Major General N. P. Banks* (Philadelphia, 1948), 3.
2 For a copy of Lincoln's letter to Secretary of War Edwin Stanton

relating to this matter, see *Private and Official Correspondence of Gen. Benjamin F. Butler During the Period of the Civil War* (Norwood, Mass., 1917), II, 587.

3 Robert U. Johnson and Clarence B. Buel (eds.), *Battles and Leaders of the Civil War* (New York, 1887), III, 586. Hereinafter cited as *Battles and Leaders.*

4 *Official Records,* XV, 886.

5 *Confederate Veteran,* VI (1898), 250. The *Dr. Beatty's* 20-pound Parrott was commanded by Captain R. M. Boone, supposedly a descendant of Daniel Boone.

6 *Ibid.,* 574.

7 The *Indianola* was later blown up by the Confederates to prevent her recapture. This removed any chance they had of organizing a naval force strong enough to protect Port Hudson and Vicksburg.

8 Cecil D. Eby, Jr. (ed.), *A Virginia Yankee in the Civil War: The Diaries of David Hunter Strother* (Chapel Hill, 1961), 152–53.

9 Richard B. Irwin, *History of the Nineteenth Army Corps* (New York, 1893) 77. For an amusing account of the review, see Eby (ed.), *A Virginia Yankee in the Civil War,* 154.

10 Wright, *Port Hudson,* 15; *Official Records,* XV, 913. For a biographical sketch of General Gardner, see Warner, *Generals in Gray,* 97. Corporal J. Wesley Powers wrote to his close friend, Linn B. Sanders, about the new commander: "I believe we have a very good general." Robert Partin, "Report of a Corporal of the Alabama First Infantry on Talk and Fighting Along the Mississippi 1862–63," *Alabama Historical Quarterly,* XX, 587.

11 Wright, *Port Hudson,* 16.

12 *Ibid.,* 6–8.

13 *Ibid.,* 17; Douglas Southall Freeman, *A Calendar of Confederate Papers* (Richmond, 1908), 357.

14 Wright, *Port Hudson,* 13.

15 In writing to his friend, Sanders, Corporal Powers stated on March 13: "We are now looking for an attack hourly." Powers was confident about the forthcoming battle. "When old Banks makes an attack on this place he will get a worse whipping than he ever had in Virginia." *Alabama Historical Quarterly,* XX (1958), 587–88.

16 Rev. James K. Ewer, *The Third Massachusetts Cavalry in the War for the Union* (Maplewood, Mass. 1903), 60.

17 Henry A. Willis, *Fitchburg in the War of the Rebellion* (Fitchburg, Mass., 1866), 77.

18 Irwin, *History of the Nineteenth Army Corps,* 78–79.

CHAPTER IV · *March 14*

1 The *Essex* was originally part of Porter's fleet, but in dueling with the *Arkansas* she ran below the Vicksburg batteries and was permanently linked with Farragut's fleet.

2 For additional details on these warships see Richard West, Jr., *Mr. Lincoln's Navy* (New York, 1957), 149–50, 218; John Randolph Spears, *David G. Farragut* (Philadelphia, 1905), 178, 180, 286; H. Allen Gosnell, *Guns on the Western Waters: The Story of River Gunboats in the Civil War* (Baton Rouge, 1949), 204, 212, 220; Francis Vinton Greene, *The Mississippi* (New York, n.d.), 215; Smith, *Company K, First Alabama Regiment*, 48; Fletcher Pratt, *The Navy: A History* (New York, 1941), 225, 424, 425, 428; Richard S. West, Jr., *The Second Admiral: A Life of David Dixon Porter 1813–1891* (New York, 1937), 175; Edgar Stanton Maclay, *A History of the United States Navy from 1775 to 1898* (New York, 1899), 140; Jim Dan Hill, *Sea Dogs of the Sixties* (Minneapolis, 1935), 43; Bernon Blythe, *A History of the Civil War in the United States* (New York, 1914), 140. The combined fleet mounted 128 guns, ranging from 12-pound howitzers to 11-inch Dahlgrens.

3 Charles Lee Lewis, *David Glasgow Farragut* (Annapolis, 1943), 169–170.

4 A. T. Mahan, *Admiral Farragut* (New York, 1892), 221. Mahan suggested that this should have been done on all Federal ships.

5 Hill, *Sea Dogs of the Sixties*, 43; Lewis, *David Glasgow Farragut*, 168.

6 Mahan, *Admiral Farragut*, 208.

7 Hill, *Sea Dogs of the Sixties*, 44; Irwin, *History of the Nineteenth Army Corps*, 79.

8 Gosnell, *Guns on the Western Waters*, 206.

9 Lewis, *David Glasgow Farragut*, 170.

10 Smith, *Company K, First Alabama Regiment*, 48.

11 *Battles and Leaders*, III, 566.

12 Spears, *David G. Farragut*, 282–83.

13 Irwin, *History of the Nineteenth Army Corps*, 78–79.

14 Charles B. Boynton, *The History of the Navy During the Rebellion* (New York, 1868), II, 295.

15 Maclay, *A History of the United States Navy*, II, 375–76. The *Richmond* was the slowest ship and the *Genesee* was the fastest ship in the squadron.

16 Dudley W. Knox, *A History of the United States Navy* (New York, 1948), 255.

17 Wright, *Port Hudson,* 17.
18 *Ibid.,* 18.
19 Smith, *Company K, First Alabama Regiment,* 50. "Confederates lit great bonfires on both banks, using reflectors like those on locomotives to project the light in the manner of a modern searchlight." Knox, *A History of the United States Navy,* 256. "A number of locomotive headlights were turned on the river—the first use of search-lights on the westerly bank of the river, and threw a glare over the water by which the shore gunners were able to aim almost as well as if it were day." Spears, *David G. Farragut,* 287.
20 Boynton, *The History of the Navy During the Rebellion,* II, 297.
21 Lewis, *David Glasgow Farragut,* 176.
22 Boynton, *The History of the Navy During the Rebellion,* 297. The *Hartford* had been first to get into things. According to Dr. Thomas Beacon, who was aboard the *Richmond,* Farragut's plan (previously decided upon) was that the Yankee ships were not to return any fire from the Confederate batteries in order that they might keep their positions secret. But the *Hartford* actually was first to open fire. Clarence Edward Macartney, *Mr. Lincoln's Admirals* (New York, 1956), 60.
23 *Ibid.,* 61.
24 J. Cutler Andrews, *The North Reports the Civil War* (Pittsburgh, 1955), 389–90.
25 Frank Moore (ed.), *The Rebellion Record: A Diary of American Events With Documents, Narratives, Illustrative Incidents, Poetry, etc.* (New York, 1866), VII, 452–53.
26 Boynton, *The History of the Navy During the Rebellion,* II, 303–304.
27 Maclay, *A History of the United States Navy,* II, 373.
28 Linus Pierpont Brockett, *Battle-Field and Hospital* (New York, n.d.), 230.
29 Boynton, *The History of the Navy During the Rebellion,* II, 299–300.
30 Smith, *Company K, First Alabama Regiment,* 51.
31 Boynton, *The History of the Navy During the Rebellion,* II, 307–308.
32 *Ibid.,* 305.
33 Maclay, *A History of the United States Navy,* II, 375–76.
34 Boynton, *The History of the Navy During the Rebellion,* II, 308.
35 *Ibid.,* 309.
36 George Dewey, *Autobiography of George Dewey: Admiral of the Navy* (New York, 1913), 90–92.

37 *Ibid.,* 93.
38 Smith, *Company K, First Alabama Regiment,* 52–53. There is much confusion over what really started the fire that destroyed the *Mississippi.* Smith claims his men ignited it before abandoning ship. Confederate gunners claimed to have set her afire.
39 *Southern Historical Society Papers,* XIV (1886), 310.
40 Smith, *Company K, First Alabama Regiment,* 49–50.
41 Maclay, *A History of the United States Navy,* II, 375. See also Boynton, *The History of the Navy During the Rebellion,* II, 303, 304, 311; Spears, *A History of the United States Navy,* 256. Among the Confederates who participated in the night's action was Edward Douglass White, later Chief Justice of the United States Supreme Court, but at this time a young member of General Beall's staff. White served through the entire siege, although suffering from fever.

CHAPTER V · *Spring Lull*

1 Wright, *Port Hudson,* 16–17. Some generals like to retain all their troops under their command and dislike detaching men to other companies. Gardner may have belonged to this group.
2 Edward Young McMorries, *History of the First Regiment Alabama Volunteer Infantry, C.S.A.* (Montgomery, 1904), 57.
3 *Official Records,* XV, 268; William B. Stevens, *History of the Fiftieth Regiment of Infantry Massachusetts Volunteer Militia in the Late War of the Rebellion* (Boston, 1904), 57.
4 *Official Records,* XV, 1059, 1071–76.
5 Irwin, *History of the Nineteenth Army Corps,* 164.
6 *Official Records,* XV, 1059.
7 See D. Alexander Brown, *Grierson's Raiders* (Urbana, 1950), 5–221; Lossing, *Pictorial History of the Civil War,* II, 601–602; John C. Pemberton, *Pemberton: Defender of Vicksburg* (Chapel Hill, 1942), 101; William Robertson Garrett and Robert Ambrose Halley, *The History of North America: The Civil War from A Southern Standpoint* (Philadelphia, 1905), XIV, 375; Mark Mayo Boatner, *The Civil War Dictionary* (New York, 1959), 359–60; Henry Steele Commager, *The Blue and the Gray* (Indianapolis, 1950), II, 661; New Orleans *Daily Picayune,* July 30, 1905.
8 Wright, *Port Hudson,* 21–22.
9 *Ibid.,* 22; See Henry T. Johns, *Life With the Forty-ninth Massachusetts Volunteers* (Washington, 1890), 328.
10 Smith, *Company K, First Alabama Regiment,* 56; *Official*

Records, XXVI, Pt. 1, p. 145. This weapon was captured on the Amite River. It was mounted on a 24-pound siege carriage—a clumsy arrangement.

11 Smith, *Company K, First Alabama Regiment,* 56–57.
12 *Ibid.,* 56–58; Wright, *Port Hudson,* 22–24.
13 Johns, *Life With the Forty-ninth Massachusetts Volunteers,* 365; Wright, *Port Hudson,* 23.
14 Johns, *Life With the Forty-ninth Massachusetts Volunteers,* 328; Wright, *Port Hudson,* 23.
15 *Confederate Veteran,* VI (1898), 173.
16 Wright, *Port Hudson,* 23–24.
17 *Ibid.,* 21, 45.
18 *Official Records,* XV, 1080. "To hold Vicksburg and Port Hudson is necessary . . . to our connection with Trans-Mississippi. You may expect whatever is in my power to do for your aid." This telegram from President Jefferson Davis was received by Pemberton on May 7. Robert McElroy, *Jefferson Davis: The Unreal and the Real* (New York, 1937), 378.
19 *Official Records,* XXVI, Pt. 1, pp. 537–38.
20 *Ibid.,* 525–26; John C. Palfrey, "Port Hudson," *The Mississippi Valley Tennessee, Georgia, Alabama, 1861–1864: Papers of the Military Historical Society of Massachusetts* (Boston, 1910), VIII, 36–37.
21 *Official Records,* XXVI, Pt. 1, pp. 494–95.
22 *Ibid.,* 500.
23 *Official Records,* XXVI, Pt. 2, p. 9; Pemberton, *Pemberton: Defender of Vicksburg,* 184–85.
24 Salmon P. Chase, *Diary and Correspondence of Salmon P. Chase* (Washington, 1902, 1903), 396–97.
25 *Official Records,* XXVI, Pt. 1, p. 180.
26 New Orleans *Daily Picayune,* July 30, 1905.
27 Francis W. Preston, *Port Hudson: A History of the Investment, Siege and Capture* (Brooklyn, 1892), 22–23.
28 Irwin, *History of the Nineteenth Army Corps,* 161.

CHAPTER VI · *The Investment*

1 Wright, *Port Hudson,* 24.
2 Irwin, *History of the Nineteenth Army Corps,* 161–62.
3 Wright, *Port Hudson,* 24–25; Irwin, *History of the Nineteenth Army Corps,* 466.
4 Johns, *Life With the Forty-ninth Massachusetts Volunteers,* 214.
5 McMorries, *History of the First Regiment Alabama Volunteer Infantry,* 58.

6 *Southern Historical Society Papers,* XIV (1886), 315.
7 *Ibid.*
8 *Official Records,* XXVI, Pt. 1, pp. 165–66.
9 *Southern Historical Society Papers,* XIV, 315–16.
10 McMorries, *History of the First Regiment Alabama Volunteer Infantry,* 60.
11 *Ibid.*
12 *Ibid.*
13 *Official Records,* XV, 316; Boynton, *The History of the Navy During the Rebellion,* 321–23.
14 *Official Records,* XXVI, Pt. 1, p. 152.
15 *Ibid.,* 148–49, 169, 508.
16 Stevens, *History of the Fiftieth Regiment,* 130.
17 Preston, *Port Hudson,* 20; *Official Records,* XXVI, Pt. 1, pp. 134–39.
18 *Southern Historical Society Papers,* XIV, 316.
19 *Ibid.,* 318; McMorries, *History of the First Regiment Alabama Volunteer Infantry,* 58.
20 Wright, *Port Hudson,* 31.
21 Smith, *Company K, First Alabama Regiment,* 62; McMorries, *History of the First Regiment Alabama Volunteer Infantry,* 62; *Southern Historical Society Papers,* XIV, 318; Wright, *Port Hudson,* 26.
22 Irwin, *History of the Nineteenth Army Corps,* 167.
23 *Official Records,* XXVI, Pt. 1, pp. 508–509. See also pp. 84–85.
24 Irwin, *History of the Nineteenth Army Corps,* 167–68.

CHAPTER VII · *May 27*

1 Irwin, *History of the Nineteenth Army Corps,* 169. Van Zandt's brigade had formerly been commanded by General William Dwight, who was now acting as commander of a provisional division.
2 *Southern Historical Society Papers,* XIV, 319; Smith, *Company K, First Alabama Regiment,* 63. For a detailed description of the Federal advance, see George N. Carpenter, *History of the 8th Regiment, Vermont Volunteers* (Boston, 1886), 114–15.
3 Irwin, *History of the Nineteenth Army Corps,* 170–71; *Southern Historical Society Papers,* XIV, 320.
4 McMorries, *History of the First Regiment Alabama Volunteer Infantry,* 64. The shot was deflected by a rib and came out the back. Captain Steedman soon recovered and returned to active duty during the siege.

5   *The Record of Athol, Massachusetts, In Suppressing the Great Rebellion* (Boston: 1886), 99–100.
6   Benjamin Quarles, *The Negro in the Civil War* (Boston, 1953), 216.
7   Irwin, *History of the Nineteenth Army Corps,* 170.
8   Otis F. R. Waite, *New Hampshire in the Great Rebellion* (Claremont, N.H., 1870), 380–81; Stevens, *History of the Fiftieth Regiment,* 154.
9   Irwin, *History of the Nineteenth Army Corps,* 171–72. Johnson's regiment held a line three quarters of a mile long. The Arkansans had only 292 men to hold the whole line. See Wright, *Port Hudson,* 34; Smith, *Company K, First Alabama Regiment,* 63.
10 William E. S. Whitman and Charles H. True, *Maine in the War for the Union: A History of the Part Borne by Maine Troops in the Suppression of The American Rebellion* (Lewiston, Maine, 1865), 294; Smith, *Company K, First Alabama Regiment,* 63.
11 *Southern Historical Society Papers,* XIV, 320. The "Bull Pen" was located roughly between Commissary Hill and Fort Desperate. A line of entrenchments ran through the field which was enclosed within the Bull Pen. The Tenth Arkansas probably was on the left of this.
12 McMorries, *History of the First Regiment Alabama Volunteer Infantry,* 61; *Southern Historical Society Papers,* XIV, 320.
13 The Negro troops were the First and Third Louisiana Native Guards. The Second Louisiana Native Guards were not at Port Hudson. The Second Louisiana Infantry, which fought bravely in the May 27 assault, was composed of white troops. The First Louisiana Guard was composed of free men of color and was under the command of Lieutenant Colonel Chauncy J. Bassett. The field officers of the regiment were whites, but according to George W. Williams, *A History of the Negro Troops in the Rebellion: 1861–1865* (New York, 1888), 216, the line officers were all free men of color. According to Irwin, *History of the Nineteenth Army Corps,* 174, the line officers were whites who had taken over on the resignation of the free men of color. The Third Louisiana Native Guards was under the command of Lieutenant Colonel Henry Finnegas (Colonel John A. Nelson was in command of a demi-brigade composed of the two guard regiments and the supporting white troops). The Third contained a few free men of color, but most of the troops were former slaves. All the officers—line and field—were white. Williams, *Negro Troops in the Rebellion,* 216. The combined strength of the two regiments was 1,080 men. Joseph T. Wilson, *The Black Phalanx: A History of the Negro Soldier of the United States in the War*

of 1775–1812, 1861–65 (Hartford, 1888), 526. According to Kettell, *History of the Great Rebellion,* II, 753, the regiments numbered 1,800.

14 Irwin, *History of the Nineteenth Army Corps,* 172–73.

15 *Southern Historical Society Papers,* XIV, 321.

16 Irwin, *History of the Nineteenth Army Corps,* 173; Wilson, *The Black Phalanx,* 213. Wilson reported that Shelby had twelve guns. The report of the twelve field pieces has been mentioned in other Northern accounts. It is not true. See Quarles, *The Negro in the Civil War,* 216.

17 There were 2,000 white troops in support. Crawford M. Jackson, "An Account of the Occupation of Port Hudson," *Alabama Historical Quarterly* XVIII (1956), 476.

18 Charles P. Bossom, *History of the Forty-second Regiment Infantry, Massachusetts Volunteers* (Boston, 1886), 361.

19 *Southern Historical Society Papers,* XIV, 321–22; Wilson, *The Black Phalanx,* 526. The Parrott was in Battery No. I; the Columbiads in Batteries No. IV and V.

20 Irwin, *History of the Nineteenth Army Corps,* 174; *Southern Historical Society Papers,* XIV, 322. The Native Guards drove to within "pistol shot of the fortifications," when they were stopped not by Confederate fire but by a back flow of the Mississippi River. The Guards attempted to ford the "backwash," but only thirty-five or forty succeeded in crossing. "This handful actually followed their reckless leader (Captain Quinn) up to the very cannon's mouth, and for 15 or 20 minutes held the whole rebel battery in their hands." Seeing their danger, Finnegas ordered the troops' retreat. Wilson, *The Black Phalanx,* 525. This is a fairy tale which gained much credence in the North. Many Union accounts speak of repeated charges of the two regiments. There were three charges according to Lossing, *Pictorial History of the Civil War,* II, 632; Quarles, *The Negro in the Civil War,* 218–19. Dudley Taylor Cornish, *The Sable Arm* (New York, 1956), 142, spoke of six or more charges, as did Williams, *Negro Troops in the Rebellion,* 219.

21 John Robertson, *Michigan in the War* (Lansing, 1882), 267.

22 *Harper's Weekly,* July 18, 1863.

23 New Orleans *Daily True Delta,* June 24, 1863. The casualties for the First Regiment were 2 officers and 24 men killed, and 79 men wounded. The Third Regiment lost 1 officer and 5 men killed, and 1 officer wounded. The total for the two regiments was 112 casualties. Irwin, *History of the Nineteenth Army Corps,* 174. Other Northern accounts differ considerably. According to Wilson, *The Black Phalanx,* 526, 371 men were killed and 150

wounded, while 16 were listed as missing. Quarles, *The Negro in the Civil War,* 220, gives 37 dead, 155 wounded, and 116 missing. Williams, *Negro Troops in the Rebellion,* 219, gives the losses of the two regiments "after six desperate charges," as 37 dead, 155 wounded, and 16 missing. Kettell, *History of the Great Rebellion,* II, 753, states that the official returns "did not, however, show a heavy loss." Assuming that each colored regiment numbered 540 men, the First Louisiana Native Guard suffered 20 per cent losses in the attack. In the same attack the Eighth New Hampshire lost 41.6 per cent casualties. During the June 14 assault the Fourth Wisconsin suffered 63 per cent casualties among the troops engaged.

24 New Orleans *Daily True Delta,* August 18, 1863.

25 *Southern Historical Society Papers,* XIV, 322. This is from Shelby's official report. My estimate is based upon company rolls.

26 Moore (ed.), *The Rebellion Record,* VII, 210.

27 *Official Records,* Ser. II, Vol. VI, 177, 631; Moore (ed.), *The Rebellion Record,* VII, 210.

28 Johns, *Life With the Forty-ninth Massachusetts Volunteers,* 257. The Negroes had stated before the battle that they were planning to kill any Confederate prisoners they took. L. Carroll Root, "The Experiences of A Federal Soldier in Louisiana," *Louisiana Historical Quarterly,* XIX (1936), 658.

29 Smith, *Company K, First Alabama Regiment,* 63.

30 Wright, *Port Hudson,* 35–36.

31 New Orleans *Daily True Delta,* September 16, 1863.

32 Lossing, *Pictorial History of the Civil War,* II, 633. This poem by an unidentified writer appeared in the Albany *Evening Journal.*

33 Irwin, *History of the Nineteenth Army Corps,* 174–77.

34 Neal Dow, *The Reminiscences of Neal Dow: Recollections of Eighty Years* (Portland, 1898), 689–91. Sherman was not the only one to oppose the attack. General Dow felt "that it would result only in the useless sacrifice of life." *Ibid.,* 689. Augur had expressed himself as being opposed to the assault at the council the night of May 26. Palfrey, "Port Hudson," *loc. cit.,* 39.

35 Irwin, *History of the Nineteenth Army Corps,* 176.

36 Kettell, *History of the Great Rebellion,* II, 752. Apparently after this attempt, there was no further effort at establishing communications between the two divisions.

37 Irwin, *History of the Nineteenth Army Corps,* 176–77.

38 Johns, *Life With the Forty-ninth Massachusetts Volunteers,* 225.

39 *Southern Historical Society Papers,* XIV, 324.

40 *Confederate Veteran,* XVI (1908), 428.

41 G. G. Benedict, *Vermont in the Civil War: A History of the Part Taken by the Vermont Soldiers and Sailors in the War For the Union 1861–65* (Burlington, n.d.), II, 177, 714.

42 Dow, *Reminiscences of Neal Dow,* 690–93.

43 Wickham Hoffman, *Camp, Court, and Siege* (New York, 1877), 70; *Arkansas Historical Quarterly,* XI (1952), 313; Dow, *Reminiscences of Neal Dow,* 692.

44 *Official Records,* XXVI, Pt. 1, pp. 124–25; Irwin, *History of the Nineteenth Army Corps,* 177; George Phister, *New York in the War of the Rebellion 1861–65* (Albany, 1912), V, 3920.

45 John Smith Kendall, "Recollections of a Confederate Officer," *Louisiana Historical Quarterly,* XXIX (1946), 1114.

46 Irwin, *History of the Nineteenth Army Corps,* 178; *Official Records* XXVI, Pt. 1, pp. 124–25; Edward Bacon, *Among the Cotton Thieves* (Detroit, 1867), 136; "I have heard before of negroes turning white from fright, and did not believe it; but it is literally true." Hoffman, *Camp, Court, and Siege,* 74.

47 Waite, *New Hampshire in the Great Rebellion,* 524. See New Orleans *Daily True Delta,* June 16, 1863, for an account written by a correspondent of the New York *Tribune.* See also issue of July 12, 1863; Hoffman, *Camp, Court, and Siege,* 71.

48 Lawrence Van Alstyne, *Diary of an Enlisted Man* (New Haven, 1910), 115.

49 Dow, *Reminiscences of Neal Dow,* 693–95.

50 *Ibid.,* 695; Irwin, *History of the Nineteenth Army Corps,* 178–79; *Southern Historical Society Papers,* XIV, 324.

51 Lossing, *Pictorial History of the Civil War,* II, 634.

52 *Confederate Veteran,* XVI (1908), 428.

53 *Southern Historical Society Papers,* XIV, 324.

54 *Louisiana Historical Quarterly,* XXIX (1946), 1117.

55 Wright, *Port Hudson,* 33. The Twenty-third Arkansas helped fight off the Zouaves. They had a busy day helping fend off attacks from Grover's and Sherman's divisions. Some of them perhaps even helped ward off Augur.

56 Whitman and True, *Maine in the War,* 325.

57 Irwin, *History of the Nineteenth Army Corps,* 179–80.

58 Kettell, *History of the Great Rebellion,* II, 752. The First Indiana was formerly the Twenty-first Infantry.

59 Johns, *Life With the Forty-ninth Massachusetts Volunteers,* 228.

60 Albert Plummer, *History of the Forty-eighth Massachusetts Volunteer Militia During the Civil War* (Boston, 1907), 37. Half of O'Brien's men carried either fascines or cotton bags to breach the ditch in front of the Confederate works.

61 Johns, *Life With the Forty-ninth Massachusetts Volunteers,* 228–29.
62 *Ibid.*
63 Plummer, *History of the Forty-eighth Massachusetts,* 39.
64 Johns, *Life With the Forty-ninth Massachusetts Volunteers,* 235, 238. On May 27, 1862, Chapin had been wounded while serving under McClellan on the Peninsula. At Port Hudson he led the charge in full-dress uniform, a good target for the Confederates. As Chapin fell, his troops began to falter.
65 *Ibid.,* 233–34. The Confederates were so struck with Bartlett's reckless courage that orders were issued not to shoot him. Kettell, *History of the Great Rebellion,* II, 753; Johns, *Life With the Forty-ninth Massachusetts Volunteers,* 233–34. Bartlett was simply so close to the Confederate lines that he was hit by accident. His wooden leg possibly caused him to lose his balance.
66 *Southern Historical Society Papers,* XIV, 325; Smith, *Company K, First Alabama Regiment,* 64, 142.
67 Smith, *Company K, First Alabama Regiment,* 64.
68 *Ibid.*
69 *Southern Historical Society Papers,* XIV, 325; Smith, *Company K, First Alabama Regiment,* 65; Lossing, *Pictorial History of the Civil War,* II, 633. One Union account gives Confederate losses for May 27 at 600 men. Kettell, *History of the Great Rebellion,* II, 753. In comparing casualties of the Union and Confederate sides as a whole, the Confederate losses were small.
70 *Official Records,* XXVI, Pt. 1, pp. 47, 68. These figures concur with Colonel Richard Irwin's. The colored troops' casualties given by Irwin also represent the official Union casualty list. The official casualties of the First and Third Louisiana Native Guards are given as 180 men; however, this figure includes losses for the entire siege.
71 Phister, *New York in the War,* V, 3921; Willis, *Fitchburg in the War of the Rebellion,* 83; *The Record of Athol, Massachusetts,* 100; Wright, *Port Hudson,* 58; Waite, *New Hampshire in the Great Rebellion,* 381; *Southern Historical Society Papers,* XIV, 325.
72 Palfrey, "Port Hudson," *loc. cit.,* 42.
73 *Official Records,* XXVI, Pt. 1, p. 509.
74 Harrington, *Fighting Politician,* 121.
75 *Official Records,* XXVI, Pt. 1, p. 509.
76 Moore (ed.), *The Rebellion Record,* VII, 43. See Frank M. Flinn, *Campaigning With Banks in Louisiana '63 and '64 and with Sheridan in the Shenandoah Valley in '64 and '65* (Lynn, Mass.: 1887), 165.

CHAPTER VIII · *Spade and Cannon*

1 Palfrey, "Port Hudson," *loc. cit.,* 42.
2 Smith, *Company K, First Alabama Regiment,* 66–67. Lieutenant L. A. Schirmer was in command of the Parrott. *Official Records,* XXVI, Pt. 1, p. 153.
3 Banks's headquarters was a deserted mansion filled with "fine looking quadroon and mulatto girls" to take care of the domestic work. Bacon, *Among the Cotton Thieves,* 131.
4 Irwin, *History of the Nineteenth Army Corps,* 185.
5 George G. Smith, *Leaves from A Soldier's Diary: The Personal Record of Lieutenant George G. Smith of Co. C., 1st La. Reg. Inf. Volunteers During the War of the Rebellion* (Putnam, 1906), 66. Lieutenant Smith was a Union Officer at Port Hudson. He recorded the incident and I have no reason to doubt his veracity. When a flag of truce is in effect, both sides are expected not to engage in any sort of military operations, including the construction of fortifications. Gardner sent Banks the following dispatch on May 28, 1863: "General: I am informed that your troops are erecting a battery within easy range on my left. As this work could be materially interfered with if I should open on them, I consider it a violation of the truce." *Official Records,* XXVI, Pt. 1, p. 515; Moore (ed.), *The Rebellion Record,* VII, 268.
6 Caroline E. Whitcomb, *History of the Second Massachusetts Battery of Light Artillery 1861–65* (Concord, 1912), 48.
7 Wright, *Port Hudson,* 37; Smith, *Company K, First Alabama Regiment,* 66.
8 The Confederates possessed two breech-loading guns, probably Whitworths, manned by a detachment of Wingfield's Battalion. *Southern Historical Society Papers,* XIV, 326.
9 Elias P. Pellet, *A History of the 114th Regiment New York State Volunteers* (Norwich, N.Y., 1866), 91.
10 *Official Records,* XXVI, Pt. 1, 520, 523; Irwin, *History of the Nineteenth Army Corps,* 186–87.
11 Wright, *Port Hudson,* 38; *Confederate Veteran,* VIII (1900), 230; Smith, *Company K, First Alabama Regiment,* 65.
12 Smith, *Company K, First Alabama Regiment,* 67–68.
13 Wright, *Port Hudson,* 39.
14 Smith, *Company K, First Alabama Regiment,* 68–69.
15 *Ibid.,* 69. Apparently the Confederates could not depress the muzzles of the Columbiads enough to hit the main Union line, but some damage was done to their second line.

16 William F. Tiemann, *The 159th Regiment Infantry, New York State Volunteers in the War of the Rebellion, 1862–65* (Brooklyn, 1891), 43; Homer B. Sprague, *History of the 13th Infantry Regiment of Connecticut Volunteers, During the Great Rebellion* (Hartford, 1867), 143.

17 A considerable supply of powder was being sent to General Edmund Kirby Smith, but the powder was at Port Hudson when the siege began, so Gardner made good use of it. Palfrey, "Port Hudson," *loc. cit.,* 57–58.

18 *Louisiana Historical Quarterly,* XXIX (1946), 1113.

19 Sprague, *History of the 13th Infantry Regiment,* 142; Plummer, *History of the Forty-eighth Massachusetts,* 65; Tiemann, *The 159th Regiment Infantry,* 43. Captain Scott Todd, Forty-eighth Massachusetts, was struck in the mouth by an old piece of French bayonet—three inches long—which knocked out his front teeth, cut his tongue in two, and stuck in the roof of his mouth. He recovered and eventually returned to duty. Plummer, *History of the Forty-eighth Massachusetts,* 65–66.

20 *Official Records,* XXVI, Pt. 1, pp. 153–55.

21 *Ibid.,* 100.

22 *Ibid.*

23 *Louisiana Historical Quarterly,* XXIX (1946), 1118.

24 One Confederate soldier, standing on the summit of the river bluff drinking a mug of beer, was killed by a Minié ball. John William DeForest, *A Volunteer's Adventures: A Union Captain's Record of the Civil War* (New Haven, 1946), 122.

25 *Official Records,* XXVI, Pt. 1, p. 171.

26 *Louisiana Historical Quarterly,* XXIX (1946), 1124.

27 McMorries, *History of the First Regiment Alabama Volunteer Infantry,* 65–66.

28 *Louisiana Historical Quarterly,* XXIX (1946), 1124.

29 DeForest, *A Volunteer's Adventures,* 122.

30 Waite, *New Hampshire in the Great Rebellion,* 181–82.

31 Sprague, *History of the 13th Infantry Regiment,* 143.

32 DeForest, *A Volunteer's Adventures,* 121.

33 *Ibid.,* 122.

34 George H. Hepworth, *The Whip, Hoe, and Sword: The Gulf Department of 1863* (Boston, 1864), 293–94. According to one Federal Soldier, the Confederates employed telescopic sights on some of their rifles, enabling them to pick off Federals at very great ranges. Van Alstyne, *Diary of an Enlisted Man,* 134.

35 Carpenter, *History of the 8th Regiment, Vermont Volunteers,* 119.

36 Stevens, *History of the Fiftieth Regiment,* 162.

37 Plummer, *History of the Forty-eighth Massachusetts,* 40.
38 Frank L. Byrne, *Prophet of Prohibition: Neal Dow and His Crusade* (Madison, 1961), 96.
39 *Official Records,* XXVI, Pt. 1, pp. 134–35. See Whitcomb, *History of the Second Massachusetts Battery,* 49.
40 New Orleans *Daily Picayune,* July 30, 1905; *Confederate Veteran,* XIII (1905), 122–23; *Official Records,* XXVI. Pt. 1, pp. 135, 181.
41 Preston, *Port Hudson,* 25–26. A large quantity of rum was found and the cavalrymen drank it freely.
42 Irwin, *History of the Nineteenth Army Corps,* 192.
43 Carpenter, *History of the 8th Regiment, Vermont Volunteers,* 121–22; Pellett, *A History of the 114th Regiment,* 108–109; DeForest, *A Volunteer's Adventures,* 127–31.
44 DeForest, *A Volunteer's Adventures,* 132.
45 *Official Records,* XXVI, Pt. 1, p. 873.
46 *Louisiana Historical Quarterly,* XXIX (1946), 1124; Wright, *Port Hudson,* 47. As a consequence of Pruyn's return to Port Hudson with Johnston's message, it was realized by the Confederate garrison that help was probably not forthcoming and that they were on their own.
47 Wright, *Port Hudson,* 39–40; *Official Records,* XXVI, Pt. 1, pp. 552–53.
48 *Alabama Historical Quarterly,* XVIII (1956), 475.
49 *Official Records,* XXVI, Pt. 1, p. 553.
50 Bacon, *Among the Cotton Thieves,* 148.
51 Waite, *New Hampshire in the Great Rebellion,* 525.
52 Plummer, *History of the Forty-eighth Massachusetts,* 41–42.
53 Smith, *Company K, First Alabama Regiment,* 248. This may have been an earthquake.
54 Irwin, *History of the Nineteenth Army Corps,* 194.
55 *Ibid.,* 194–95.

CHAPTER IX · *June 14*

1 Smith, *Company K, First Alabama Regiment,* 64–65.
2 Palfrey, "Port Hudson," *loc. cit.,* 43.
3 Wright, *Port Hudson,* 36; Smith, *Company K, First Alabama Regiment,* 65; McMorries, *History of the First Regiment Alabama Volunteer Infantry,* 64.
4 Colonel Sidney A. Bean, who had led the regiment so gloriously on May 27, was killed on May 29.
5 Waite, *New Hampshire in the Great Rebellion,* 382.
6 Preston, *Port Hudson,* 33. The ditch was shallow enough to per-

mit the infantry to cross without the cotton-bag bridge, but the artillery needed the crude bridge in order to pass over the ditch. Whitcomb, *History of the Second Massachusetts Battery*, 50.

7 Lossing, *Pictorial History of the Civil War*, II, 635. Colonel Currie had served with the British in the Crimean War. See Irwin, *History of the Nineteenth Army Corps*, 203.

8 *Southern Historical Society Papers*, XIV, 328; Smith, *Company K, First Alabama Regiment*, 71.

9 Preston, *Port Hudson*, 34.

10 *Southern Historical Society Papers*, XIV, 328.

11 Willis, *Fitchburg in the War of the Rebellion*, 88. Paine's men penetrated through the gap under cover of the fog which had not yet lifted. *Southern Historical Society Papers*, XIV, 328.

12 George W. Powers, *The Story of the Thirty-eighth Regiment of Massachusetts Volunteers* (Cambridge, 1866), 107–108.

13 *Southern Historical Society Papers*, XIV, 328; Waite, *New Hampshire in the Great Rebellion*, 383.

14 *Southern Historical Society Papers*, XIV, 328.

15 Preston, *Port Hudson*, 36–37.

16 *Official Records*, XXVI, Pt. 1, p. 147.

17 *Southern Historical Society Papers*, XIV, 328–29.

18 *Louisiana Historical Quarterly*, XIX (1936), 666; Kettell, *History of the Great Rebellion*, II, 756; DeForest, *A Volunteer's Adventures*, 134.

19 DeForest, *A Volunteer's Adventures*, 134.

20 Sprague, *History of the 13th Infantry Regiment*, 148.

21 *Louisiana Historical Quarterly*, XIX (1936), 666.

22 DeForest, *A Volunteer's Adventures*, 133.

23 *Ibid.*, 135.

24 Weitzel's attack was directed against the right face of the Priest Cap, but his division somewhat overlapped the mark and part of it hit the section of works held by the Fifteenth Arkansas. Some portion of the First Alabama moved down to reinforce the two beleaguered Confederate regiments. The Confederates had approximately six hundred men engaged against Weitzel and Paine.

25 Phister, *New York in the War*, I, 128. Two other brothers, twins, lost their lives in defense of the Port Hudson garrison. And a few days later "an exploding shell gave a death wound to the heart-broken father." West Baton Rouge *Sugar Planter*, February 17, 1866.

26 Pellet, *A History of the 114th Regiment New York State Volunteers*, 118–19.

27 *Louisiana Historical Quarterly*, XIX (1936), 667.

28 Kettell, *History of the Great Rebellion*, II, 757; Harris H.

Beecher, *Record of the 114th Regiment N.Y.S.V. Where it Went, What it Saw, and What it Did* (Norwich, N.Y., 1866), 205–206.

29 James Franklin Titts, "A June Day at Port Hudson," *Galaxy*, II (1866), 129.

30 Beecher, *Record of the 114th Regiment N.Y.S.V.*, 205.

31 Sprague, *History of the 13th Infantry Regiment*, 150–51. Colonel Morgan commanded the First Brigade on June 14, but sometime before the brigade went into action, Holcomb, First Louisiana, assumed command of the brigade and Morgan took command of the division, Birge having assumed command of Paine's division.

32 Newspaper clipping dated August 7, 1897, in Simon Jerrard Papers, Louisiana State University Archives.

33 Sprague, *History of the 13th Infantry Regiment*, 152–55.

34 *Ibid.*, 156–57. For his words Jerrard was dishonorably dismissed from the United States Army. See *Official Records*, XXVI, Pt. 1, pp. 589–90; Simon Jerrard Papers, Louisiana State University Archives; *General Orders 1863, Department, Army Corps and Division*, Captain Frederic Speed, Assistant General U.S.V.

35 Sprague, *History of the 13th Infantry Regiment*, 157.

36 Johns, *Life With the Forty-ninth Massachusetts Volunteers*, 287.

37 *Ibid.*, 289.

38 *Confederate Veteran*, X (1902), 317–18.

39 Irwin, *History of the Nineteenth Army Corps*, 194; *Official Records*, XXVI, Pt. 1, p. 14.

40 *Official Records*, XXVI, Pt. 1, p. 549. Captain W. W. Wheeler, Sixth Michigan, said Dwight was intoxicated when he issued the order. Bacon, *Among the Cotton Thieves*, 153–56. Staff and regimental officers claimed that Dwight was drunk during the actual assault. See Charles Lanmon, *The Red Book of Michigan: A Civil, Military and Biographical History* (Detroit, 1871), 334.

41 Bacon, *Among the Cotton Thieves*, 151–57; *Official Records*, XXVI, Pt. 1, p. 549.

42 Waite, *New Hampshire in the Great Rebellion*, 525–26. The bridge over the gully had already been destroyed.

43 *Ibid.*, 526.

44 Irwin, *History of the Nineteenth Army Corps*, 200.

45 John S. C. Abbott, "Siege and Capture of Port Hudson," *Harper's New Monthly* (1865), 436

46 Johns, *Life With the Forty-ninth Massachusetts Volunteers*, 292.

47 Irwin, *History of the Nineteenth Army Corps*, 197; Stevens, *History of the Fiftieth Regiment*, 178.

48 Preston, *Port Hudson*, 44. Darkness fell before a party of stretcher-bearers was able to rescue General Paine.

49 John Truesdale, *The Blue Coats* (Philadelphia, 1867), 136.

50 Charles P. Roland, *Louisiana Sugar Plantations During the American Civil War* (Leiden, 1957), 62; Stevens, *History of the Fiftieth Regiment,* 190.

51 James K. Hosmer, *The Color Guard: A Corporal's Notes of Military Service in the Nineteenth Army Corps* (Boston, 1864), 178–80.

52 Hoffman, *Camp, Court, and Siege,* 70.

CHAPTER X · *Grim Days*

1   *Official Records,* XXVI, Pt. 1, p. 56.

2   DeForest, *A Volunteer's Adventures,* 144–45.

3   *Ibid.*

4   William Fowler, Sr., *Memorials of William Fowler* (New York, 1875), 44–45; Beecher, *Record of the 114th Regiment N.Y.S.V.,* 209.

5   Van Alstyne, *Diary of an Enlisted Man,* 133.

6   Johns, *Life With the Forty-ninth Massachusetts Volunteers,* 303.

7   DeForest, *A Volunteer's Adventures,* 145.

8   Irwin, *History of the Nineteenth Army Corps,* 212–13; Sprague, *History of the 13th Infantry Regiment,* 166.

9   *Official Records,* XXVI, Pt. 1, p. 557.

10 Wright, *Port Hudson,* 42–43.

11 Smith, *Company K, First Alabama Regiment,* 72.

12 Bacon, *Among the Cotton Thieves,* 186. Colonel Bacon was a bitter enemy of Dwight, but the statement is probably correct, as there were other witnesses. A Southern girl who lived nearby was later to recall: "The stench became so terrible that we could scarcely breathe, especially at night." Mrs. S. G. Miller, *Sixty Years in the Nueces Valley* (San Antonio, 1930), 203.

13 Kettell, *History of the Great Rebellion,* II, 758. In collecting the Union dead, the Confederates found a wounded flyblown Yankee captain. He was turned over to the Federal medical personnel and he recovered. See Smith, *Company K, First Alabama Regiment,* 72; Wright, *Port Hudson,* 43.

14 *Southern Historical Society Papers,* XIV, 333.

15 Willoughby Babcock, Jr., *Selections From the Letters and Diaries of Brevet-Brigadier General Willoughby Babcock of the 75th New York Volunteers* (New York, 1922), 95. General Babcock overheard an incident relating to the racial issue. A Southerner yelled, "Hello! Yank, Get down there. I want to shoot that damned nigger."

16 Hoffman, *Camp, Court, and Siege*, 72–73. According to De-Forest, *A Volunteer's Adventures*, 144, the Twelfth Connecticut had no informal truces. "Every day we shot at each other across the ravine from morning to night."

17 Carpenter, *History of the 8th Regiment, Vermont Volunteers*, 131.

18 Bacon, *Among the Cotton Thieves*, 215. Union officers had told their men that Gardner refused to permit a flag of truce for taking care of the Union wounded who fell June 14.

19 The Twenty-fourth Connecticut fired an average of 4,000 cartridges a day during 25 days on the firing line. W. A. Croffut and John H. Morris, *The Military and Civil History of Connecticut During the War of 1861–63* (New York, 1868), 419.

20 Carpenter, *History of the 8th Regiment, Vermont Volunteers*, 130.

21 *Louisiana Historical Quarterly*, XXIX (1946), 1127.

22 *The Bivouac: An Independent Military Monthly*, (Boston, 1894), II, 121.

23 *Confederate Veteran*, XVII (1909), 69.

24 Carpenter, *History of the 8th Regiment, Vermont Volunteers*, 131.

25 Hosmer, *The Color Guard*, 210.

26 Whitcomb, *History of the Second Massachusetts Battery*, 51–52.

27 Smith, *Company K, First Alabama Regiment*, 77.

28 West Baton Rouge *Sugar Planter*, February 24, 1866.

29 *Confederate Veteran*, XVII (1909), 512.

30 *Ibid.*

31 McMorries, *History of the First Regiment Alabama Volunteer Infantry*, 67.

32 *Alabama Historical Quarterly*, XVIII (1956), 476.

33 R. S. McClung, "Three Years in the C.S. Army (P.A.C.S.)" (Original diary, University of Texas Library), 9.

34 Beecher, *Record of the 114th Regiment N.Y.S.V.*, 198.

35 *Official Records Atlas* (Washington, 1891–95), plate 38.

36 Bacon, *Among the Cotton Thieves*, 209, 228.

37 *Ibid.*, 225. The soldiers on the firing line with only a few inches of dirt for protection, called Dwight's command post "the safe," and indeed it was safe from artillery and sharpshooter fire.

38 Irwin, *History of the Nineteenth Army Corps*, 211.

39 *Official Records Atlas*, plate 38. Grover's men were assigned the task against Fort Desperate, or the "Bastion," as the Federals called it.

40 Bacon, *Among the Cotton Thieves*, 274; *Confederate Veteran*,

XXXVI (1929), 136. Major Bailey struck one sick black with a pickax when the contraband refused to work. Bacon, *Among the Cotton Thieves,* 225.

41 Wright, *Port Hudson,* 46.

42 Whitman and True, *Maine in the War for the Union,* 543.

43 Wright, *Port Hudson,* 46.

44 Palfrey, "Port Hudson," *loc. cit.,* 52–53.

45 *Ibid.* Fascines were long bundles of sticks used for fortifying the saps and batteries. Gabions were simply containers filled with dirt used for fortifications. A sap roller was a large gabion which the sapper rolled before him for protection from the fire of the enemy.

46 Irwin, *History of the Nineteenth Army Corps,* 221.

47 *Confederate Veteran,* VI (1898), 444; Wright, *Port Hudson,* 46; Smith, *Company K, First Alabama Regiment,* 73.

48 Hosmer, *The Color Guard,* 213; Irwin, *History of the Nineteenth Army Corps,* 223.

49 Wright, *Port Hudson,* 44.

50 *Official Records,* XXVI, Pt. 1, p. 161.

51 This description is based upon a study of the maps concerning the siege, the present geographical location of the Priest Cap, and the surrounding works. Union and Confederate accounts substantially agree with this.

52 Babcock, *Selections From the Letters and Diaries,* 31.

53 Palfrey, "Port Hudson," *loc. cit.,* 60.

54 *Confederate Veteran,* VIII (1900), 230.

55 Wright, *Port Hudson,* 50; Palfrey, "Port Hudson," *loc. cit.,* 60. Captain Palfrey stated that the mine was not seriously damaged.

56 *Official Records,* XXVI, Pt. 1, pp. 149–50. The Arkansans spiked the guns of one battery. Smith, *Company K, First Alabama Regiment,* 73.

57 Taylor was not seriously considering New Orleans, but the Federals did not know this. Taylor did capture Brashear City on June 23, and succeeded in cutting off Banks's communications from New Orleans by planting a battery on the Mississippi River. For a more detailed description in regard to Port Hudson, see Richard Taylor, *Destruction and Reconstruction* (New York, 1955).

58 Van Alstyne, *Diary of an Enlisted Man,* 147.

59 *Ibid.,* 136.

60 Wright, *Port Hudson,* 44.

61 DeForest, *A Volunteer's Adventures,* 133; Sprague, *History of the 13th Infantry Regiment,* 172.

62 Bacon, *Among the Cotton Thieves,* 287; DeForest, *A Volunteer's Adventures,* 138.

63 *Confederate Veteran,* V (1897), 513. Jordan was killed a few days later. A shell burst near him, tearing off his right leg and severing his backbone.

64 *Official Records,* XXVI, Pt. 1, p. 155. Colonel De Gournay made special mention of Schirmer's bravery in his official report. Schirmer was twenty-four years old, of Danish nationality, and had fought at the siege of Sevastopol with the British. *Confederate Veteran,* XXX (1922), 55.

65 *Official Records,* XXVI, Pt. 1, p. 151.

66 Van Alstyne, *Diary of an Enlisted Man,* 140.

67 *Official Records,* XXVI, Pt. 1, pp. 150–51.

68 Bacon, *Among the Cotton Thieves,* 260–61.

69 *Louisiana Historical Quarterly,* XXIX (1946), 1128. The Citadel was called Battery No. XI or the "Devil's Elbow" by the Confederates.

70 *Official Records,* XXVI, Pt. 1, p. 151; Lanmon, *The Red Book of Michigan,* 334.

71 Sergeant Abram E. Garrison to his wife, letter dated August 27, 1863, Abram E. Garrison Papers, Michigan Historical Collection, University of Michigan.

72 *Confederate Veteran,* XIII (1905), 31–32.

73 *Louisiana Historical Quarterly,* XXIX (1946), 1119.

74 Bacon, *Among the Cotton Thieves,* 229, 277.

75 *Louisiana Historical Quarterly,* XIII (1905), 1122.

76 McMorries, *History of the First Regiment Alabama Volunteer Infantry,* 67.

77 Palfrey, "Port Hudson," *loc cit.,* 58–59.

78 *Official Records,* XXVI, Pt. 1, p. 165.

79 Wright, *Port Hudson,* 49.

80 Bacon, *Among the Cotton Thieves,* 263.

CHAPTER XI · *The End*

1 Fowler, *Memorials of William Fowler,* 44–45, 52.

2 Plummer, *History of the Forty-eighth Massachusetts,* 49.

3 *Official Records,* XXVI, Pt. 1, p. 565.

4 Stevens, *History of the Fiftieth Regiment,* 191.

5 *Official Records,* XXVI, Pt. 1, p. 14.

6 Pellet, *A History of the 114th Regiment,* 127.

7 Stevens, *History of the Fiftieth Regiment,* 195.

8 Johns, *Life With the Forty-ninth Massachusetts Volunteers,* 301.

Some of the nine-month troops who mutinied were imprisoned in the Dry Tortugas or on Ship Island. Charles Henry Moulton to his sister, letter dated July 15, 1863, Moulton Papers, Michigan Historical Collections, University of Michigan.

9   Stevens, *History of the Fiftieth Regiment,* 195.

10 Johns, *Life With the Forty-ninth Massachusetts Volunteers,* 301.

11 Plummer, *History of the Forty-eighth Massachusetts,* 45. Not all of the nine-month troops were unwilling to serve. The Sixteenth New Hampshire and several others were willing to remain on duty until the siege ended. Luther Tracy Townsend, *History of the Sixteenth Regiment, New Hampshire Volunteers* (Washington, 1897), 243. The Sixteenth New Hampshire was on duty guarding the ammunition depot and Banks's headquarters and not on the firing line.

12 Bacon, *Among the Cotton Thieves,* 252; *Official Records,* XXVI, Pt. 1, 560, 599. The acting lieutenant colonel of the Sixth Michigan stated that Bacon was arrested "for saying to soldiers that he did not believe we could take Port Hudson by assault and other things which he ought not to have said." Eli Augustus Griffin to his wife, letter dated June 27, 1863, Griffin Papers, Michigan Historical Collections, University of Michigan.

13 Bacon, *Among the Cotton Thieves,* 270–77.

14 Waite, *New Hampshire in the Great Rebellion,* 520. The Confederates experienced some disciplinary problems and disharmony, the difference being that while the Yanks wanted to quit fighting and go home, the Southerners—especially the Arkansans —wanted to start shooting and fight their way out of Port Hudson. Colonel Vaughan, Tenth Arkansas, was relieved of his command and replaced by Captain S. M. Shelton. The Arkansans, although brave, lacked discipline.

15 Ewer, *The Third Massachusetts Cavalry,* 95–97; New Orleans *Daily Picayune,* July 30, 1905; Moore (ed.), *The Rebellion Record,* VII, 6.

16 *Official Records,* XXVI, Pt. 1, p. 559.

17 New Orleans *Daily Picayune,* July 30, 1905; Moore (ed.), *The Rebellion Record,* VII, 6; Irwin, *History of the Nineteenth Army Corps,* 215. Irwin reported the Union loss at 100 prisoners. Pascoe reported 700 captured.

18 Bacon, *Among the Cotton Thieves,* 280.

19 Hosmer, *The Color Guard,* 200–203.

20 *Ibid.;* Pellet, *A History of the 114th Regiment,* 127; Ellen Louise Power, "Diary, January 1, 1862– September 28, 1863" (Original in University of North Carolina Library), 80. Banks's Order No. 50, issued from Port Hudson, stated that contrabands were to

be exclusively used as teamsters, enabling the white troops to do combat duty. The engagement took place at the Keller plantation. According to Hosmer, if it had not been for the cannon, "We might all have been on the way to Richmond." Hosmer, *The Color Guard,* 203. Confederate losses were seven wounded and none killed. "Power Diary," 80.

21 "Power Diary," 80; Ewer, *The Third Massachusetts Cavalry,* 359–61. Private William A. Jackuish, Co. A, Third Massachusetts Cavalry, wrote an article entitled "Confiscating Cotton at Port Hudson," in which he told of an expedition to the Shalmire Plantation near Springfield Landing. The Yankees confiscated all the corn and cotton, leaving the family with nothing to eat. Thousands of bales of cotton were confiscated during the siege, of which only a few bales were used in the actual fighting. What happened to the rest is still a mystery.

22 John McGrath Scrapbook, John McGrath Papers, Louisiana State University Archives. General Dow himself, in his *Reminiscences of Neal Dow,* gave a different version of his capture. But McGrath had occasion to talk to most of the participants, and his account is presumably more accurate.

23 *Official Records,* XXVI, Pt. 1, p. 72. According to Townsend's *History of the Sixteenth New Hampshire,* 250, the black troops of Ullman's Corps d'Afrique broke and ran for the river, along with many teamsters, servants, etc. In the panic "two negroes rushed into the river and were drowned"; a disaster was barely averted as the Sixteenth New Hampshire formed behind the levee and stopped the mob with fixed bayonets. *Official Records,* XXVI, Pt. 1, p. 73.

24 New Orleans *Daily Picayune,* July 30, 1863; Johns, *Life With the Forty-ninth Massachusetts Volunteers,* 307. Several days later a party of Federal cavalry rode into the landing. Someone yelled, "Rebels! The Rebs is comin'." *Official Records,* XXVI, Pt. 1, p. 73. The contrabands, hearing the cry, panicked, and a wild stampede ensued in which many ran into the river and 21 were drowned. Johns, *Life With the Forty-ninth Massachusetts,* 307.

25 New Orleans *Daily Picayune,* July 30, 1905. Irwin put Union losses at one killed, eleven wounded, and twenty-one captured or missing. Irwin, *History of the Nineteenth Army Corps,* 216. The Freeman house, near the town of Wilson, is still standing.

26 *Official Records,* XXVI, Pt. 1, p. 182. Logan speaks of leading the raid; however, Powers may have led the attack. See "Power Diary," 81.

27 "Power Diary," 81; Ewer, *The Third Massachusetts Cavalry,* 334–35.

28 *Arkansas Historical Quarterly*, XI (1956), 312.
29 Irwin, *History of the Nineteenth Army Corps*, 226.
30 Townsend, *History of the Sixteenth New Hampshire*, 279.
31 Irwin, *History of the Nineteenth Army Corps*, 227.
32 Wright, *Port Hudson*, 54; *Alabama Historical Quarterly*, XVIII (1956), 477.
33 Smith, *Company K, First Alabama Regiment*, 78. Crawford M. Jackson said Colonel Johnson was present at this council meeting. *Alabama Historical Quarterly*, XVIII (1956), 477. According to a Confederate officer, it was seriously considered that the Confederates should cut their way through Banks's army and link up with Logan. This was probably rejected because it would have necessitated leaving some 3,000 sick and wounded Southerners to the tender mercies of the Yanks. Kendall, *Louisiana Historical Quarterly*, XXIX (1946), 1129.
34 *Official Records*, XXVI, Pt. 1, pp. 52–54.
35 McMorries, *History of the First Regiment Alabama Volunteer Infantry*, 69.
36 Irwin, *History of the Nineteenth Army Corps*, 231.
37 *Louisiana Historical Quarterly*, XXIX (1946), 1132.
38 *Alabama Historical Quarterly*, XVIII (1956), 479–80. Jackson ran into several Federal officers who wanted to detain him as a drinking partner and not because he was suspected of being a Confederate. One officer called to Jackson, "Hold! We have some fine brandy here; get down and join us, and tell us how many of the rebs we have captured." After drinking to their health Jackson bade them farewell and rode on.
39 McMorries, *History of the First Regiment Alabama Volunteer Infantry*, 102, 108.
40 Smith, *Company K, First Alabama Regiment*, 80.
41 Sprague, *History of the Thirteenth Infantry Regiment*, 171. "Col. Lee was one of the few rebel officers who never drank a drop of liquor," wrote Sprague. This statement could apply to either army with real justification.
42 Johns, *Life With the Forty-ninth Massachusetts Volunteers*, 325.
43 Beecher, *Record of the 114th Regiment N.Y.S.V.*, 225.
44 Johns, *Life With the Forty-ninth Massachusetts Volunteers*, 325.
45 Townsend, *History of the Sixteenth New Hampshire*, 286–87.
46 Sprague, *History of the Thirteenth Infantry Regiment*, 171.
47 Townsend, *History of the Sixteenth New Hampshire*, 289.
48 Smith, *Company K, first Alabama Regiment*, 82–83.
49 *Ibid.; Official Records*, Ser. II, Vol. VI, 232. This is from a dispatch from Halleck to Banks.

50 *Official Records,* Ser. II, Vol. VI, 147.

51 W. Brewer, *Alabama: Her History, Resources, War Record and Public Men* (Montgomery, 1872), 590.

52 *Louisiana Historical Quarterly,* XXIX (1946), 1132–35. Kendall escaped from the Customs House on July 31. Three captains, W. H. Smith, William H. Davidson, and T. J. Nicholson, escaped from custody shortly afterwards. These three were from the Forty-ninth Alabama. Brewer, *Alabama,* 663.

53 *Official Records,* XXVI, Pt. 2, p. 10.

54 *Ibid.,* XXVI, Pt. 1, p. 147.

55 *Ibid.,* XXVI, Pt. 2, 98.

56 *Ibid.,* XXVI, Pt. 1, p. 631.

57 *Ibid.,* 144. Logan and Powers lost from 40 to 50 men killed or wounded during the campaign.

58 The highest estimate of the Union army is nearly 45,000 men, in Kettell, *History of the Great Rebellion,* II, 751. Other estimates were 20,000 men as of June 12: Bacon, *Among the Cotton Thieves,* 129; Harrington, *Fighting Politician,* 120. There were 30,000 troops according to Benedict, *Vermont in the Civil War,* II, 123. Greene estimated 30,700 in *The Mississippi,* 228. These figures exclude the Baton Rouge garrison. The Confederate casualty returns include Logan's cavalry.

59 Grierson's cavalry had a special six-gun battery which had been brought from LaGrange, Tennessee. The Yankees had two machine guns at Port Hudson. Van Alstyne, *Diary of an Enlisted Man,* 122. These probably were Ellsworth guns which had been brought to Louisiana with Butler's expedition. Benedict, *Vermont in the Civil War,* II, 99.

60 This is computed on the basis of the returns of five regiments selected at random—Twenty-eighth New Hampshire, Fifteenth New Hampshire, Twenty-fourth Maine, and the Forty-eighth and Fiftieth Massachusetts.

61 *Official Records,* XXVI, Pt. 1, p. 611.

62 Benedict, *Vermont in the Civil War,* II, 84, 135. The July 1 morning report for the Eighth Vermont showed an aggregate of 732 men present, and by adding the 209 casualties suffered in the previous fighting, the total is 941.

63 Tiemann, *The 159th Regiment Infantry,* 132.

64 Irwin, *History of the Nineteenth Army Corps,* 219. The June 30 returns showed 1,585 men as the aggregate present. See *Official Records,* XXVI, Pt. 1, p. 611.

65 Irwin, *History of the Nineteenth Army Corps,* 219: *Official Records,* XXVI, Pt. 1, p. 611.

66 *Official Records,* XXVI, Pt. 1, pp. 527–28. According to returns from Banks's headquarters for the month of May, 1863, the United States Army had 30,916 men present for duty at Port Hudson, an aggregate present of 37,666, and a total of 47,620 present and absent. These figures exclude the garrison at New Orleans, but presumably include the garrisons at Baton Rouge, Donaldsonville, Brashear City, and Butte à la Rose.

67 *Ibid.,* 611.

68 The monthly returns listed all Louisiana commands (including Port Hudson) together, except those under Grierson and Ullman, and part of those under Emory. This report stated that 32,423 men were present for duty, that there was an aggregate present of 39,770 men, and a total of 49,766 present and absent. *Official Records,* XXVI, Pt. 1, p. 610.

69 Irwin claimed 17,000 men, excluding Grierson's cavalry, was the largest number of troops at Port Hudson on any single day. He said the number of reinforcements received totaled only about 3,000. Irwin, *History of the Nineteenth Army Corps,* 216. His figures in the *Official Records* radically differ, but he explained this by saying May and June returns were the March returns carried forward. He was undoubtedly mistaken for the April 30 returns from the army at Opelousas showed 33,529 men present for active duty in Louisiana. See *Official Records,* XV, 711. Irwin wrote his account thirty years after the event and his memory may have failed him.

70 Johns, *Life With the Forty-ninth Massachusetts Volunteers,* 317.

71 DeForest, *A Volunteer's Adventures,* 103.

72 General Dow was not satisfied with his troops' taking the temperance pledge, but spent much time roaming around the camps smashing liquor bottles. Harrington, *Fighting Politician,* 118. See Bacon, *Among the Cotton Thieves,* 120–294, for numerous incidents concerning Union generals and junior officers who spent their time looting civilians, drinking, or associating with loose women. See Ludwell Johnson, *Red River: Cotton and Politics in the Civil War* (Baltimore, 1958), for further adventures of some of Banks's generals.

73 Fitzgerald Ross, *Cities and Camps of the Confederate States* (Urbana, 1958), 215.

74 Johns, *Life With the Forty-ninth Massachusetts Volunteers,* 302.

75 Babcock, *Selections From the Letters and Diaries,* 82. Most of the Confederate arms at the beginning of the siege before the Yankee rifles were captured were old style smoothbore muskets —often of the old Queen Bess pattern—not one in ten having a

bayonet. Johns, *Life With the Forty-ninth Massachusetts Volunteers*, 325. Many of the muskets were old flintlocks imported from Europe through the blockade. The cartridge for close work held 12 to 15 buckshot. Bacon, *Among the Cotton Thieves*, 285.

76 Wright, *Port Hudson*, 52; Stevens, *History of the Fiftieth Regiment*, 207. These guns would only fire once because the recoil would knock them off the blocks.

Bibliography

OFFICIAL RECORDS AND DOCUMENTS

Everhart, William C. *Vicksburg: National Military Park, Mississippi.* Washington, D.C.: National Park Service Historical Handbook, Series No. 21, 1954.

General Orders 1863, Department, Army Corps and Divisions. Captain Frederick Speed, Assistant Adjutant General U.S.V., Washington, D.C.: Government Printing Office, 1863.

Lattimore, Ralston B. *Fort Pulaski: National Monument.* Washington, D.C.: National Park Service Handbook, Series No. 18, 1914.

U.S. Navy Department. *The War of the Rebellion: Official Records of the Union and Confederate Navies.* 30 vols. Washington, D.C.: 1894–1922.

U.S. War Department. *War of the Rebellion: Atlas to Accompany the Official Records of the Union and Confederate Armies.* Compiled by Calvin D. Cowles. 175 plates. Washington, D.C.: 1891–95. New edition. *Official Atlas of the Civil War.* Edited by Henry Steele Commager. New York: Thomas Yoseloff, Inc., 1958.

U.S. War Department. *The War of the Rebellion: A Compilation of the Official Records of the Union and Confederate Armies.* 128 vols. Washington, D.C.: 1880–1901.

UNPUBLISHED MATERIALS

Brown, Harry Bates, Jr. "Port Hudson: A Study in Historical Geography." M.A. Thesis, Louisiana State University, 1936.

Abram E. Garrison Papers, Michigan Historical Collections, University of Michigan.

Eli Augustus Griffin Papers, Michigan Historical Collections, University of Michigan.

Simon Jerrard Papers, Louisiana State University Archives.

McClung, R. S. "Three Years in the C.S. Army (P.A.C.S.)." Original manuscript, University of Texas Library.

John McGrath Papers, Louisiana State University Archives.

Charles Henry Moulton Papers, Michigan Historical Collections, University of Michigan.

161

Nash, William H. "Fiftieth Regiment Massachusetts Volunteer Company D Diary for 1863." Typescript copy of original manuscript, Louisiana Department, Louisiana State Library.
Power, Ellen Louise. "Diary, January 1, 1862–September 28, 1863." Original manuscript, University of North Carolina Library.

NEWSPAPERS AND PERIODICALS

Bivouac: An Independent Military Monthly, II, 1884.
Confederate Veteran, 40 vols., January, 1893–December, 1932.
Galaxy, II (September 15, 1866).
Harper's New Monthly, XXX (March, 1865).
Harper's Weekly, VII (July 18, 1863).
New Orleans Daily Picayune, July 30, 1905.
New Orleans Daily True Delta, June 16–September 16, 1863.
New Orleans Times-Democrat, April 26, 1906.
West Baton Rouge Sugar Planter, February 17, 24, 1866.

ARTICLES IN PERIODICALS

Bonham, Milledge L., Jr., "Man and Nature at Port Hudson," Military Historian and Economist, II (October, 1917).
Frederick, J. V. (ed.), "War Diary of W. C. Porter," Arkansas Historical Quarterly, XI (1952), 286–314.
Jackson, Crawford M., "An Account of the Occupation of Port Hudson, Louisiana," Alabama Historical Quarterly, XVIII (October, 1956), 474–85.
Kendall, John Smith, "Recollections of a Confederate Officer," Louisiana Historical Quarterly, XXIX (October, 1946), 1041–1228.
Partin, Robert, "Report of a Corporal of the Alabama First Infantry on Talk and Fighting Along the Mississippi 1862–63," Alabama Historical Quarterly, XX (October, 1958), 583–94.
Root, L. Carroll, "The Experiences of A Federal Soldier in Louisiana," Louisiana Historical Quarterly, XIX (October, 1936), 635–67.

BIOGRAPHIES

Byrne, Frank L. Prophet of Prohibition: Neal Dow and His Crusade. Madison, Wisconsin: University of Wisconsin Press, 1961.
Harrington, Fred Harvey. Fighting Politician: Major General N. P. Banks. Philadelphia: University of Pennsylvania Press, 1948.
Lewis, Charles Lee. David Glasgow Farragut. Annapolis: United States Naval Institute, 1943.
Mahan, A. T. Admiral Farragut. New York: D. Appleton and Company, 1892.

Pemberton, John C. *Pemberton: Defender of Vicksburg.* Chapel Hill: University of North Carolina Press, 1942.

Spears, John Randolph. *David G. Farragut.* Philadelphia: George W. Jacobs and Company, 1905.

West, Richard S., Jr. *The Second Admiral: A Life of David Dixon Porter, 1813–1891.* New York: Coward-McCann, Inc., 1937.

STATE AND LOCAL HISTORIES

Benedict, G. G. *Vermont in the Civil War: A History of the Part Taken by the Soldiers and Sailors in the War for the Union 1861–65.* 2 vols. Burlington, Vermont: The Free Press Association, 1886–88.

Brewer, W. *Alabama: Her History, Resources, War Record and Public Men.* Montgomery: Barrett and Brown, 1872.

Croffut, W. A. and John M. Morris. *The Military and Civil History of Connecticut During the War of 1861–65.* New York: Ledyard Bell, 1868.

Lanmon, Charles. *The Red Book of Michigan: A Civil, Military and Biographical History.* Detroit: E. B. Smith and Company, 1871.

Lindsey, John Berrien. *The Military Annals of Tennessee.* Nashville: J. M. Lindsey and Company, 1866.

Phister, George. *New York in the War of the Rebellion 1861–65.* 5 vols. Albany: L. B. Lyon Company, 1912.

The Record of Athol, Massachusetts, in Suppressing the Great Rebellion. Boston: George C. Rand and Avery, 1866.

Robertson, John. *Michigan in the War.* Lansing, W. S. George and Company, 1882.

Rowland, Dunbar. *The Official and Statistical Register of the State of Mississippi.* Nashville: Brandon Publishing Company, 1908.

Skipwith, H. *East Feliciana, Louisiana: Past and Present.* New Orleans: Hopkins Printing Office, 1892.

Waite, Otis F. R. *New Hampshire in the Great Rebellion.* Claremont, N.H.: Tracy, Chase and Company, 1870.

———. *Vermont in the Rebellion.* Claremont, N.H.: Tracy, Chase and Company, 1869.

Whitman, William E. S. and Charles H. True. *Maine in the War for the Union: A History of the Part Borne by Maine Troops in the Suppression of the American Rebellion.* Lewiston, Maine: Nelson Dingley, Jr. and Company, 1865 .

Willis, Henry A. *Fitchburg in the War of the Rebellion.* Fitchburg, Mass.: Stephen Shepley, 1866.

PERSONAL NARRATIVES AND DIARIES

Babcock, Willoughby, Jr. *Selections From the Letters and Diaries of Brevet-Brigadier General Willoughby Babcock of the 75th New York Volunteers.* New York: University of the State of New York, 1922.

Bacon, Edward. *Among the Cotton Thieves.* Detroit: The Free Press Steam Book and Job Printer House, 1867.

Cannon, J. P. *Inside of Rebeldom: The Daily Life of A Private in the Confederate Army.* Washington, D.C.: The National Tribune, 1900.

Chase, Salmon P. *Diary and Correspondence of Salmon P. Chase.* Washington: American Historical Association Annual Report for the year 1902–1903.

Dawson, Sarah Morgan. *A Confederate Girl's Diary.* New edition. Bloomington: University of Indiana Press, 1960.

DeForest, John William. *A Volunteer's Adventures: A Union Captain's Record of the Civil War.* New Haven: Yale University Press, 1946.

Dewey, George. *Autobiography of George Dewey: Admiral of the Navy.* New York: Charles Scribner's Sons, 1913.

Dow, Neal. *The Reminiscences of Neal Dow, Recollections of Eighty Years.* Portland, Maine: The Evening Express Publishing Company, 1898.

Eby, Cecil D., Jr. (ed.). *A Virginia Yankee in the Civil War: The Diaries of David Hunter Strother.* Chapel Hill: University of North Carolina Press, 1961.

Flinn, Frank M. *Campaigning With Banks in Louisiana in '63 and '64 and with Sheridan in the Shenandoah in '64 and '65.* Lynn, Mass.: Press of Thomas P. Nichols, 1887.

Hepworth, George H. *The Whip, Hoe, and Sword: The Gulf Department of 1863.* Boston: Walker, Wise and Company, 1864.

Hoffman, Wickham. *Camp, Court and Siege.* New York: Harper and Brothers, 1877.

Hosmer, James K. *The Color Guard: A Corporal's Notes of Military Service in the Nineteenth Army Corps.* Boston: Walker, Wise and Company, 1864.

Long, E. B. (ed.). *Ulysses S. Grant: Personal Memoirs.* New York: World Publishing Company, 1952.

McManus, Thomas. *Battle Fields of Louisiana Revisited a Second Time.* Hartford: The Fowler and Miller Company, 1897.

Miller, Mrs. S. G. *Sixty Years in the Nueces Valley.* San Antonio: Naylor Printing Company, 1930.

Preston, Francis W. *Port Hudson: A History of the Investment, Siege and Capture.* Brooklyn: 1892.

Private and Official Correspondence of Gen. Benjamin F. Butler During the Period of the Civil War. Vol. II. Norwood, Mass.: The Plimpton Press, 1917.

Ross, Fitzgerald. *Cities and Camps of the Confederate States.* Urbana: University of Illinois Press, 1958.

Taylor, F. Jay (ed.). *Reluctant Rebel: The Secret Diary of Robert Patrick 1861–1865.* Louisiana State University Press, 1959.

Taylor, Richard. *Destruction and Reconstruction.* New edition. New York: Longmans, Green and Company, 1955.

Van Alstyne, Lawrence. *Diary of an Enlisted Man.* New Haven: The Tuttle Morehouse and Taylor Company, 1910.

Wright, Lieutenant Howard C. *Port Hudson: Its History From an Interior Point of View.* Baton Rouge: Committee for the Preservation of the Port Hudson Battlefield, 1961.

GENERAL WORKS

Anderson, Charles C. *Fighting by Southern Federals.* New York: The Neale Publishing Company, 1912.

Andrews, J. Cutler. *The North Reports the Civil War.* Pittsburgh: University of Pennsylvania Press, 1955.

Blythe, Vernon. *A History of the Civil War in the United States.* New York: The Neale Publishing Company, 1914.

Boatner, Mark Mayo. *The Civil War Dictionary.* New York: David McKay Company, Inc., 1959.

Boynton, Charles B. *The History of the Navy During the Rebellion.* 2 vols. New York: D. Appleton and Company, 1868.

Brockett, Linus Pierpont. *Battle-Field and Hospital.* New York: Union Publishing Company, n.d.

Catton, Bruce. *This Hallowed Ground: The Story of the Union Side of the Civil War.* Garden City: Doubleday and Company, 1956.

Commager, Henry Steele. *The Blue and the Gray.* 2 vols. Indianapolis: Bobbs-Merrill Company, 1950.

Cornish, Dudley Taylor. *The Sable Arm.* New York: Longmans, Green and Company, 1956.

Dowdey, Clifford. *The Land They Fought For, The Story of the South as the Confederacy 1832–1865.* Garden City: Doubleday and Company, Inc., 1955.

Dufour, Charles L. *The Night the War Was Lost.* Garden City: Doubleday and Company, 1960.

Freeman, Douglas Southall. *A Calendar of Confederate Papers.* Richmond: The Confederate Museum, 1908.

Garrett, William Robertson and Robert Ambrose Halley. *The History of North America: The Civil War From A Southern Standpoint.* Vol. XIV. Philadelphia: George Barrie and Sons, 1905.

Gosnell, H. Allen. *Guns on the Western Waters: The Story of River Gunboats in the Civil War.* Baton Rouge: Louisiana State University Press, 1949.

Greene, Francis Vinton. *The Mississippi.* New York: Jack Brussel, Publisher, n.d.

Guernsey, Alfred H. and Henry M. Alden. *Harper's Pictorial History of the Civil War.* 2 vols. Chicago: Star Publishing Company, 1894.

Henry, Robert Selph. *The Story of the Confederacy.* New York: The New Home Library, 1936.

Hill, Jim Dan. *Sea Dogs of the Sixties.* Minneapolis: University of Minneapolis Press, 1935.

Johnson, Ludwell. *Red River Campaign: Cotton and Politics in the Civil War.* Baltimore: Johns Hopkins Press, 1958.

Johnson, Robert U. and Clarence B. Buel (eds.). *Battles and Leaders of the Civil War. Being for the Most Part Contributions by Union and Confederate Officers.* 4 vols. New York: The Century Company, 1887.

Kettell, Thomas P. *History of the Great Rebellion.* 3 vols. San Francisco: H. H. Brancroft and Company, 1863.

Knox, Dudley W. *A History of the United States Navy.* Revised edition. New York: G. P. Putnam's Sons, 1948.

Livermore, William Roscoe. *The Story of the Civil War, A Concise Account of the War in the United States of America Between 1861 and 1865.* New York: The Knickerbocker Press, 1913.

Lossing, Benson J. *Pictorial History of the Civil War in the United States of America.* 3 vols. Hartford: T. Belknap Company, 1869.

Macartney, Clarence Edward. *Mr. Lincoln's Admirals.* New York: Funk and Wagnalls Company, 1956.

McElroy, Robert. *Jefferson Davis: The Unreal and the Real.* Vol II. Harper and Brothers, 1937.

Maclay, Edgar Stanton. *A History of the United States Navy from 1775 to 1898.* New York: D. Appleton and Company, 1899.

Merrill, James M. *The Rebel Shore: The Story of Union Sea Power in the Civil War.* Boston: Little, Brown and Company, 1957.

Miers, Earl Schenck. *The Web of Victory: Grant at Vicksburg.* New York: Alfred A. Knopf, 1955.

Moore, Frank (ed.). *The Rebellion Record: A Diary of American Events with Documents, Narratives, Illustrative Incidents, Poetry, etc.* Vol. VII. New York: D. Van Nostrand, 1866.

Palfrey, John C. "Port Hudson," *The Mississippi Valley, Tennessee, Georgia, Alabama, 1861–1864: Papers of the Military Historical Society of Massachusetts.* Vol. VIII. Boston: The Military Historical Society of Massachusetts, Cadet Armory, 1910.

Pratt, Fletcher. *Civil War on Western Waters.* New York: Holt, 1956.
————. *The Navy: A History, The Story of A Service in Action.* New York: Garden City Publishing Company, Inc., 1941.

Quarles, Benjamin. *The Negro in the Civil War.* Boston: Little, Brown and Company, 1953.

Roland, Charles P. *Louisiana Sugar Plantations During the American Civil War.* Leiden: E. J. Brill, 1957.

Southern Historical Society Papers. 51 vols. Richmond: 1876–1959.

Spears, John R. *History of the United States Navy.* London: Vickers and Sons, 1898.

Teeney, Jewett W. *The Military and Naval History of the Rebellion in the U.S., with Biographical Sketches of Deceased Officers.* New York: D. Appleton and Sons, 1866.

Truesdale, John. *The Blue Coats.* Philadelphia: Jones Brothers and Company, 1867.

Warner, Ezra J. *Generals in Gray: Lives of the Confederate Commanders.* Baton Rouge: Louisiana State University Press, 1959.

West, Richard., Jr. *Mr. Lincoln's Navy.* New York: Longmans, Green and Company, 1957.

Wiley, Bell I. *The Life of Billy Yank.* Indianapolis: The Bobbs-Merrill Company, 1955.

Williams, George W. *A History of the Negro Troops in the War of the Rebellion 1861–65.* New York: Harper and Brothers, 1888.

Wilson, Joseph T. *The Black Phalanx: A History of the Negro Soldiers of the United States in the Wars of 1775, 1812, 1861–65.* Hartford: American Publishing Company, 1888.

UNIT HISTORIES

Beecher, Harris H. *Records of the 114th Regiment N.Y.S.V., Where it Went, What it Saw, and What it Did.* Norwich, N.Y.: J. F. Hubbord, Jr., 1866.

Bossom, Charles P. *History of the Forty-second Massachusetts Volunteers.* Boston: Mills, Knight and Company, 1886.

Brown, D. Alexander. *Grierson's Raiders.* Urbana: University of Illinois Press, 1950.

Carpenter, George N. *History of the 8th Regiment, Vermont Volunteers.* Boston: Press of Deland and Barta, 1886.

Ewer, Rev. James K. *The Third Massachusetts Cavalry in the War for the Union.* Maplewood, Mass.: Published by Direction of the Historical Committee of the Regimental Association, 1903.

Fowler, William, Sr. *Memorials of William Fowler.* New York: Anson D. F. Randolph and Company, 1875.

Harper, John, *et al. Rolls of the Adams Light Infantry*. Natchez, Miss.: Published by the Memorial Souvenir Committee, 1890.

Irwin, Richard B. *History of the Nineteenth Army Corps*. New York: G. P. Putnam's Sons, 1893.

Johns, Henry T. *Life With the Forty-ninth Massachusetts Volunteers*. Washington, D.C.: Ramsey and Bisbee, Printers, 1890.

McMorries, Edward Young. *History of the First Regiment Alabama Volunteer Infantry, C.S.A.* Montgomery: The Brown Printing Company, 1904.

Pellet, Elias P. *A History of the 114th Regiment New York State Volunteers*. Norwich, N.Y.: Telegraph and Chronicle Power Press Print Company, 1866.

Plummer, Albert. *History of the Forty-eighth Regiment Massachusetts Volunteer Militia During the Civil War*. Boston: Press of the New England Druggist Publishing Company, 1907.

Powers, George W. *The Story of the Thirty-eighth Regiment Massachusetts Volunteers*. Cambridge: Dakin and Metcalf, 1866.

Smith, Daniel P. *Company K, First Alabama Regiment, Three Years in the Confederate Service*. Prattville, Ala.: Published by the Survivors, 1885.

Smith, George G. *Leaves From a Soldier's Diary. The Personal Record of Lieutenant George G. Smith of Co. C, 1st La. Reg. Inf. Volunteers During the War of the Rebellion*. Putnam, Conn.: Published by the Author, 1906.

Sprague, Homer B. *History of the 13th Infantry Regiment of Connecticut Volunteers During the Great Rebellion*. Hartford: Case, Lockwood and Company, 1867.

Stevens, William B. *History of the Fiftieth Regiment of Massachusetts Volunteer Militia in the Late War of the Rebellion*. Boston: Stillings Press, 1907.

Tiemann, William F. *The 159th Regiment Infantry, New York State Volunteers in the War of the Rebellion, 1862–1865*. New York: William F. Tiemann, Publisher, 1891.

Townsend, Luther Tracy. *History of the Sixteenth Regiment New Hampshire Volunteers*. Washington, D.C.: Norman T. Elliott.

Whitcomb, Caroline E. *History of the Second Massachusetts Battery of Light Artillery, 1861–1865*. Concord: The Rumford Press, 1912.

Index